ROADKILL
COOKING
FOR
CAMPERS

CHARLES G. IRION

IRION BOOKS

www.irionbooks.com
www.roadkillcookingforcampers.com

ISBN 978-0-615-29836-8

Published by
Irion Books
4462 E. Horseshoe Rd.
Phoenix, AZ 85028

Cover Design by Jason Crye

Printed and bound in the United States of America

Contents

Introduction

Having been the owner and operator of many R.V. parks over the past 30 years, I have heard it all. Well, as much as campers talk, the truth is that I'll never hear it all, no matter how long I listen. But I've heard a lot. Stories, lies, truths, tales, rumors – and recipes. Some of those recipes have been culinary road maps to some damn weird dishes. Bear Paw Stroganoff, Pickled Muskrat and Dumplings, Haymakers Switchel, Deep Fried Lamprey, Jellied Pheasant. Oh, and Fricasseed Whistle Pig. And Jim Fancy Rabbit. That's just a sample. All sorts of roadkill recipes are included in this collection: over 350 of 'em!

Sometimes I find it hard to believe you could even think of eating some of the critters that these recipes say are supposed to go into the pot or the frying pan. These beasts, reptiles and fowl are intimidating enough skulking around out in the wild, let alone flopped on a cutting board, ready for seasoning. Still, here they are!

Some of these dishes, I'm told, are actually tasty. Some may turn your stomach a little, but that's the risk a roadkill cook always takes.

I don't want this culinary adventure to end here. If you have a weird recipe that you think would add to this collection, please send it to me (go to www.roadkillcookingforcampers.com for more info). I may include it in the next edition of the book. Who knows? If it is included, you will receive a free, signed copy of *Roadkill Cooking for Campers*. Now that's a tasty idea, isn't it?

I

Big GAme Delights

BEAR PAW
STROGANOFF

BEAR PAW STROGANOFF

4 bear paws
1 c. moose milk (or cow's milk)
1 lb. bear burger
1 onion, minced
salt
garlic
Madeira wine
1 c. onion soup (canned)
1 lb. mushrooms

Prepare bear paws by removing hide and claws. Soak in salt solution 48 hrs. at 75 degs. or less. Rinse in cold water. Simmer for 6 days, being careful to add water to keep paws covered. Change water for first 4 days every 6 hrs. The last 2 days do not use any water, but substitute a good Madeira wine. The 6th day sauté bear burger, onion, crushed garlic, and mushrooms. When browned, add moose milk (may substitute 1 c. sour cream diluted with 1/2 c. homogenized milk) and undiluted onion soup, or any soup you prefer. Salt and pepper to taste. Serve over hot, buttered noodles. Serves 4-6 or several dozen who know what they are eating for the first time.

BEAR GREASE

Bear fat rendered out makes fine cooking oil, base for medicines, etc.

BEAR CRACKLING

Crackling from rendering bear fat makes good addition to vegetables, soups, salads, bread dough, or just eat it like potato chips.

BEAR POT ROAST

4 lbs. shoulder roast
2 T. flour
1/4 c. soy sauce
3 T. bacon drippings
1/4 tsp. pepper
1/2 c. water
1 med. onion, sliced
1/4 tsp. ground ginger
1 8-oz. can drained pineapple chunks
1/3 c. chopped celery
1/4 c. water

Heat drippings in Dutch oven. Brown roast well, pour off drippings. Add soy sauce, water, pepper, ginger, and onion. Cover and bake at 350 degs. about 3 hrs. or until tender. Combine celery and pineapple and add to meat. Cook about 20 mins. longer. Remove meat to heated platter. Mix together 1/4 c. water and flour and add to pot liquids. Cook and stir until thickened. Serves 8-10. Good with hot biscuits, coleslaw, fruit cobbler, and hot drink.

BONE MARROW

Marrow is a very good base for soup and gravy stock. Cut bones in sections. Split if a band saw is handy. In large pot, cook and shake and pull out marrow. Great for sickroom foods.

BEAR STEAK

5 lbs. slices center bear loin
1 1/2 T. tomato paste
1 clove garlic, crushed
dash Worcestershire sauce
3 T. butter
1 onion, chopped
3 T. minced chives
butter
1 heaping tsp. prepared mustard
salt, pepper

Marinate bear for 24 hrs. Make a paste of butter, chives, mustard, tomato paste and Worcestershire sauce. Cover a heated platter with this paste and add a thick layer of onion chopped, smothered in the butter. Season with salt and pepper. Keep platter hot; now sear steak on both sides under a high flame and broil meat as desired, rare, medium, well done. Dust with salt and pepper. Cover with plenty of butter; serve on hot platter.

TRAIL JERKY

3-5 lbs. lean game meat, round or flank, or other lean sections. Cut meat into 1 1/2" thick steaks. Now cut strips 1/4" thick by 1 1/2" wide and as long as possible, season lightly. Dry meat on racks covered with fine wire to keep out insects. Place racks in direct sun. Cover at night with plastic. After 2 days, turn. Takes 4 days, should be dark and brittle.

BIG GAME HOLIDAY MEAT BALLS

Heat meat balls in cranberry B.B.Q. sauce. (1 can jellied cranberry sauce mixed with 3/4 c. chili sauce, 3 T. brown sugar, 1 T. lemon juice). Serve as appetizers or over hot buttered noodles or rice.

FRUITED CHRISTMAS BUFFALO ROAST

Marinate 4-5 lbs. roast in Venison Marinade for 24 hrs. Remove. Dry with paper towels. Heat 2 T. oil in Dutch oven, brown meat on all sides. Add enough marinade to cover meat. Simmer covered for 2 hrs. Meantime place a package of mixed fruit in bowl with 1 1/2 c. hot water. Let stand 1 hr. or longer until meat is tender. Serve in its own juices, with fluffy rice, buttered carrots, lettuce wedges, and cold red wine.

CORNED BIG GAME MEAT

5 lbs. boned meat
1/2 c. brown sugar
1 gal. cold water
1/2 tsp. salt
1 c. salt
1/2 tsp. pepper

Dissolve dry ingredients in water, add meat, let stand 36 hrs. Place meat and brine in kettle and simmer very slowly for about 5 hrs. or until tender. Serves about 15.

BAKED STUFFED HEART

1 heart
1 c. bread crumbs
4 slices salt pork or bacon
1/4 tsp. poultry seasoning
1 1/2 c. onion, chopped
salt and pepper

Wash and trim heart, soak in salt water about 3 hrs. Roll in seasoned flour, brown in bacon drippings. Brown and crumble salt pork or bacon. Add onion, bread crumbs, poultry seasoning, salt, and pepper. Stuff warm heart and bake in slow oven or Dutch oven covered about 3 hrs. or until tender.

SWEET AND SOUR BURRO STEAK (No. 1)

        3-4 burro steaks
        6 T. cooking oil
        1 c. fruit cocktail
        1 1/2 c. brown sugar
        1 1/2 tsp. salt
        2 T. vinegar
        2 tsp. prepared mustard

Brown steaks in Dutch oven. In saucepan, thicken remaining ingredients with cornstarch. Place a layer of steak and a layer of sauce in Dutch oven. Bake at 400 degs. about 20 mins. per pound. Add water as needed or any fruit juice. Serve hot with sauce, hot sage dressing, baked potatoes, Mexican corn, and ice cream. Serves 8-10.

SWEET AND SOUR BURRO STEAK (No. 2)

        3-4 burro steaks
        1 1/2 c. brown sugar
        6 T. cooking oil
        2 tsp. prepared mustard
        1 1/2 tsp. salt
        2 T. vinegar

Brown steaks in oil, place in Dutch oven. Combine remaining ingredients as sauce. Make a layer of steak and then sauce. Bake at 400 degs. about 20 mins. per lb. Serve with sage and celery dressing, baked potatoes, hot biscuits, tossed salad, Mexican corn, and ice cream. Serves 8-10.

BUFFALO SIRLOIN TIP

4-5 lbs. roast
salt and pepper
1/2 tsp. onion salt
2 T. margarine
3 T. water

Wipe roast with vinegar-soaked cloth, rub seasoning well into meat. Add water to roast in Dutch oven. Melt margarine and pour over roast. Place in 350 deg. preheated oven for 35 mins. Turn, baste with drippings. Continue roasting and basting for 1 1/2 hrs. more. Thicken drippings for gravy.

SADDLE OF COUGAR

Remove fat from saddle of cougar, sprinkle with salt and pepper, rub well with flour. Place on rack in pan and roast at 400 degs. for 1/2 hr., reduce heat to 300 degs. and continue roasting for about 2 hrs. longer. Do not add water to pan. Several strips of bacon placed over roast helps with basting. May be marinated overnight in solution of water, vinegar, cloves, salt, and pepper.

PICKLED HEART

1 big game heart
1 tsp. salt
1 c. sugar
4 tsp. pickling spice
1 c. vinegar

Place heart in large saucepan, and add pickling spice liquid to cover. Bring to boil and continue to cook at low boil until heart is tender. Slice before you serve hot or cold.

SPICY GAME RIBS

3 8-oz. cans tomato sauce
2 T. honey
1/2 c. minced onion
1 T. lemon juice
3 T. Worcestershire sauce
1 clove garlic, minced
salt and pepper
2 tsp. dry mustard
1/2 c. chicken bouillon
1 tsp. chili powder
3 T. packed brown sugar
8 lbs. game ribs

Combine all but ribs in saucepan. Bring to boil, reduce heat, simmer uncovered 30 mins. Brush ribs with sauce. Grill 45 mins. or until tender. Baste and turn frequently. Separate ribs into serving portions. Pass the remaining sauce at the table.

PICKLED TONGUE

1 cleaned tongue
1/4 c. sugar
1 1/2 c. cider vinegar
1 med. onion, sliced
1 1/2 c. reserved tongue stock

Wrap 2 T. mixed pickling spice and 6 whole black peppers in cheesecloth. Add to liquid in 3-qt. pan of vinegar, tongue stock, sugar, and onion, bring to boil. Put skinned, cooked tongue in bowl. Pour hot pickling liquid over it. Discard spices. Chill at least 24 hrs. Serve with horse-radish or mustard. Serves 4.

COUGAR SAUSAGE (FROM PERU)

5 lbs. cougar meat, ground
salt and pepper
2 lbs. pork, ground
casings to hold ground mix sage or
    poultry seasoning

Season to taste, fill casings, tie off links if desired.

MT. LION ROAST

3-4 lbs. roast
salt and pepper
1 clove garlic, crushed
2 T. brown sugar
2 tsp. paprika
1 tsp. dry mustard
1/4 tsp. chili powder
1/8 tsp. cayenne pepper
2 T. Worcestershire sauce
1/4 c. vinegar
1 c. tomato juice
1/2 c. water

Place roast in Dutch oven or small roaster. Season with salt, pepper, and garlic. Roast about 1 hr. at 375 degs. Remove from oven and slice. Place in iron or heavy skillet. Mix 1 tsp. salt with remaining ingredients and simmer about 15 mins. Add to sliced meat and simmer about 1 hr. longer or until meat is tender. Serve with hot biscuits, hot spicy applesauce, coleslaw, and mashed yams. Serves 8-10.

COUGAR SAUSAGE

5 lbs. ground cougar meat
2 lbs. ground pork
3/4 tsp. ground sage
1 tsp. salt

Casings to hold ground mix. Mix ingredients well and season to your taste. Fill and tie off in links, if desired. May also be used as bulk sausage.

VENISON CHILI VERDE

1 lb. lean pork, 1/4" cubes
1 16-oz. can stewed tomatoes
1 lb. round steak, 1/4" cubes
2 7-oz. cans diced green chiles
2 T. flour
1/4 tsp. oregano
2 T. drippings
2 tsp. salt
1/2 c. chopped onion
2 1/2 c. water
1 clove garlic, minced

Dredge meat in flour, melt shortening in deep skillet, brown meat thoroughly. Add onion and garlic, cook until onion is soft. Add remaining ingredients, simmer covered, 1-2 hrs., stirring once in a while. Remove cover, simmer uncovered 5-10 mins. to desired consistency.

ROAST MOOSE NOSE

Remove the large gristly portion of the nose at the top, place the entire piece in hot coals. This will burn off the hair. When done, the hide will peel off. Salt and pepper to taste and you have a meal. A real delicacy of the northern tribes and trappers.

JELLIED MOOSE NOSE

The nose is a less tender part of the animal and will require long slow cooking for best results. Cut upper jaw just below the eyes. Place in a large kettle of scalding water. Parboil 45 mins. Remove, cool in cold water, pick hair off as feathers, get all hair. Place nose in fresh water with onion, a little garlic, and pickling spice, boil gently until tender. Cool in juice overnight. In morning, remove bone and cartilage. The bulb of the nose is white meat, the thin strips along the bone and jowls are dark. Slice meat thin, pack in jars and cover with juice. This will jell, when chilled, it can be sliced. Serve cold with a heavy bread, salad, and cold beer.

RED WHISKEY VENISON CHOPS

6 chops, 3/4" thick
1 tsp. hot mustard
1 onion, finely chopped
dash Worcestershire sauce
tarragon vinegar
chili sauce
1/2 c. bourbon whiskey
dash tabasco

Simmer chops and onions, covered with 1/4" tarragon vinegar in heavy skillet until chops are tender. Add remaining ingredients and stir until the mixture is thick. Cook at low heat stirring when necessary. Add more vinegar or chili sauce as needed. When sauce is thick enough, spread on chops generously. Place in shallow pan, pour bourbon over them, bake uncovered at 350 degs. 1 1/2 hrs. Baste occasionally until done, tender.

SENECA VENISON STEW

2 green peppers, chopped
1 clove garlic, pressed
2 sweet red peppers, chopped
2 T. bacon drippings
2 onions, chopped
2 lbs. venison, diced
3 large carrots, cubed
5 potatoes, diced
2 c. canned tomatoes

Cook peppers, onions, garlic in drippings 5 mins.; add meat and brown. Add water and vegetables; cook over slow fire until tender. 30 mins. before serving add 1 tsp. each oregano, sage, chili sauce, about a T. chili. powder, mix with cold water, salt to taste, heat only to blend.

VENISON BLIZZARD SOUP

4 lbs. cubed venison or other game
2 leeks, chopped
2 med. potatoes, cubed
1/2 lb. sausage
1 can stewed tomatoes
4 carrots, chopped
1 c. celery, chopped
2 onions, chopped
salt and pepper
2 T. butter

Melt butter in Dutch oven, brown sausage and venison well. Put in remaining ingredients, bring to boil, reduce heat, simmer 2 hrs. Season to taste. Serves 6 hungry hunters. Serve with warm crusty bread, sliced tomatoes, lettuce wedges, and red wine. A real good chance to use up scraps from butchering.

FRUITED POT ROAST OF VENISON

3-5 lb. roast, marinate in venison marinade for 24 hrs. Remove. Dry with paper towels. Heat 2 T. cooking oil in Dutch oven. Brown meat on all sides. Add enough marinade to cover meat. Simmer covered for 2 hrs. Meantime, place a box of mixed fruit in bowl with 1 1/2 c. hot water. Let stand 1 hr. Place fruit on top of meat, add liquid in which fruit soaked. Cover, simmer 1 hr. longer or until meat is tender. Serve in its own juice with fluffy rice, buttered carrots, lettuce wedges, red wine (cold), and hot crusty sour dough bread.

VENISON MARINADE

1 c. salad oil
1 med. onion, sliced
1 c. cider vinegar
1/2 tsp. garlic salt
1 c. dry red wine
10 peppercorns
2 T. lemon juice
1 tsp. chopped parsley

Combine all in glass or stainless steel bowl, mix well.

VENISON HASH

Use left-over venison roast or steak, grind and mix with 1 ground onion, 1/2 green pepper, 2 ribs of celery, 1 c. instant mashed potatoes (follow package directions). Bake in 350 deg. oven for 45 mins. Serve with water cress lettuce, tomato salad, hot trail bannock, good hot coffee.

VENISON SOUP

3 1/2 lbs. of venison (shot up and
less desirable pieces)
1 lb. ham or washed salt pork
1 bunch celery, some leaves
1 large onion, diced
4 med. carrots, diced
4 potatoes, diced
6 whole peppers

Chop meat in 1/2" chunks, dice vegetables, put in fairly large stew pot with just enough water to cover. Keep the lid on, and stew slowly 1 hr. Add 2 qts. boiling water, with a few blades of mace, 1/2 doz. peppers or cayenne. Boil 2 hrs. longer. Salt and strain, return liquor to the pot, stir a T. of butter, thicken with a T. of browned flour, blend into a smooth thin paste with cold water. Add a T. of walnut, catsup or mushrooms, 1 tsp. Worcestershire sauce, or steak sauce, a tumbler of Madeira or sherry wine.

VENISON SAUSAGE

4 1/2-5 lbs. lean venison
2 tsp. cayenne pepper
2 lbs. fat salt pork
1 small onion, chopped fine
5 tsp. powdered sage
juice of 1 lemon
4 tsp. salt
4 tsp. back pepper

Chop all meat fine or use sausage grinder, pack in skin, or small stone jars. Hang the skins, and set the jars tied down with bladders in a cool dry place. Fry as with any sausage, skins may be smoked.

BREADED VENISON SAUSAGE

Wipe the link sausages dry. Dip them in beaten egg, and fine bread crumbs. Put them in a frying basket and plunge into boiling fat. Cook 10 mins., serve with a garnish of toasted bread and parsley, applesauce, flapjacks.

CARIBOU STEW

1 1/2 lbs. caribou meat cubes
1 c. beef bouillon
2 T. flour
1/4 tsp. pepper
1 T. butter
4 carrots, halved lengthwise
1 T. oil
4 whole turnips, peeled
2 cloves garlic, chopped
1 14 1/2-oz. can tomatoes, drained
1 tsp. salt
1 tsp. arrow root
1 T. lemon juice
2 T. brandy
1 bay leaf
dash nutmeg
1/4 tsp. oregano

Shake meat in seasoned flour, brown in butter and oil in heavy skillet. Place meat in Dutch oven. Place remaining flour in fry pan with garlic, salt, lemon juice, bay leaf, oregano, bouillon, and pepper. Simmer until thickened. Add carrots, turnips, and tomatoes. Place in oven or over coals (450 deg. oven) 90 mins. Thicken sauce with arrow root, adding brandy, tomato juice, and nutmeg. Bring to boil and serve with stew. Any big game meat may be used.

HOPI ACORN STEW

2 lbs. elk or deer meat in bite-size
chunks
1 tsp. salt
1 c. ground corn meal

Add water to cover meat, cook until tender,
maintaic water level, add salt when tender,
separatè from stock, chop meat into small
pieces, add acorn meal. Mix thoroughly, pour
stock over, stir. Serve.

POTTED VENISON ROAST AND VEGETABLES

4 lbs. game roast
4 onions, sliced
1 T. salt
4 carrots, scraped and quartered
3/4 tsp. pepper
1 can whole tomatoes
1 clove garlic, mashed
4 potatoes, peeled, halved
2 bay leaves

Make a paste of garlic, salt and pepper; rub
into roast. Place in Dutch oven, add onion,
carrots, tomatoes around meat. Add bay leaves,
cover. Roast at 325 degs. until tender, about
3-3 1/2 hrs., adding water from the start and
maintaining water as needed. Last 45 mins. add
potatoes, last 1/2 hr. roast uncovered.

BIG HORN-DALL SHEEP ROAST

4-8 lbs. bone in or boned and rolled, tied leg
of lamb. Smoke as directed 3 hrs. to complete
cooking. Insert meat thermometer in thickest
part of round in 325 deg. oven until thermometer registers 175 degs.; for med. about 1 hr.;
1 1/2-2 hrs. if refrigerated. Carve to serve
hot. Refrigerate to serve cold thinly sliced.

ROLLED CABBAGE (PIGS IN THE BLANKETS)

3 lbs. venison sausage
2 T margarine
2 1/2 c. cooked rice
1/2 lb. salt pork, chopped fine
2 large heads cabbage (loose heads)
2 #2 cans sauerkraut
2 c. boiling water
2 tart apples
1 large onion, chopped
salt, pepper to taste

Remove core from cabbage with a sharp knife. Scald the cabbage in boiling water, Remove leaves 1 at a time as they wilt. Trim leaves from core. Fry salt pork until light brown, add chopped onion. Remove from fire immediately. In a large bowl mix sausage and rice thoroughly with onion and salt pork, and salt and pepper. Take 1 large T. of the mixture and place on a cabbage leaf. Fold the opposite ends and roll. Tuck in sides to hold. Place cabbage rolls in large roasting pan lined with left-over leaves. Sprinkle layer with sauerkraut and place one apple in the layer. Layer in pan until ingredients are used up. Cover all with leaves and kraut and tart apple, 1 c. water. Cook at 325 degs. for 2 hrs. A good substitute for sauerkraut is tomato soup. Add water as needed. (My favorite is elk sausage.)

VENISON MINCEMEAT-ELK-MOOSE

3 lbs. venison, elk or moose
8 cored, pared, chopped apples
1 lemon
1 qt. cider
3 lbs. seedless raisins
2 tsp. cinnamon
1/2 lb. currants or jar currant
  jelly
1 tsp. allspice
1 lb. back fat, ground
3 c. sugar
1 pt. grape juice
1 tsp. ground cloves
1 orange, ground
1 tsp. salt
1 lb. seeded raisins

Grind meat. Fry lightly. Combine all ingredients. Cook in large pan on low heat 2 1/2-3 hrs., or until apples are tender. Cool package as desired. May be frozen. Add 1/2 jigger brandy to each pie when baking.

SMOKED VENISON SAUSAGE

1 lb. venison (elk, buffalo, moose)
1 tsp. salt
1/2 lb. pork
1/4 tsp. poultry seasoning
1/4 tsp. pepper
1/4 c. water
1 clove garlic

Remove all fat from meat. Blend ingredients thoroughly, stuff corings. Smoke slowly 8 hrs. To cook, simmer 20 mins.

BAKED VENISON SAUSAGE

30 lbs. venison
7 T. sage
30 lbs. pork
1 tsp. salt
7 T. black pepper
6 tsp. garlic powder

Grind all meat. Mix all ingredients well to blend spices. May be frozen, packed in commercial casings or plastic bags, and hung to smoke for 1-2 weeks. A very good chance to use shot-up meat and not-so-choice pieces. A good way to use a tough buck.

OLD FASHIONED VENISON MEAT LOAF

2 lbs. ground venison
1 c. soft bread crumbs
1/2 lb. bulk sausage
1/2 c. crushed pineapple
1 tsp. salt
dash pepper
3/4 c. tomatoes
1/2 c. minced onion
3 slices of pineapple for top
1 egg, beaten
1/2 green pepper, diced fine
1/4 c. celery, chopped fine

Combine all ingredients, mold into loaf. Line loaf pan with foil, place meat in pan, cook uncovered in 350 deg. oven until done (2 hrs.). 8 portions.

DEER LIVER, CAMP STYLE

deer or other big game liver, fresh or hang
1 large onion, sliced
salt and pepper
6 slices bacon
1 T. chopped parsley
juice 1/2 lemon

Sauté onion in bacon drippings. Thinly slice 6 slices of liver, cut slices in half. Cook with onion, turn often, cook quickly. Season with salt and pepper and a few squirts of lemon juice. Sprinkle with parsley. Serve hot.

BIG GAME CHILI

2 lbs. ground game meat
1 tsp. brown sugar
1 lb. ground pork
1 c. red wine
2 large onions, chopped
2 16-oz. cans red chili beans
3 c. tomato juice
1 tsp. black pepper
1/2 tsp. oregano
1 tsp. chili powder
2 pkgs. prepared chili mix
dash tabasco

Cook ground pork about half done. Add ground meat. Cook 30 mins. over medium heat until browned with onion. Put meat and onion into large pan. Add tomato juice, oregano, chili mix, brown sugar, wine, and pepper. Simmer 2 hrs. Add beans and simmer 1 hr. longer. Add water if chili becomes dry. Serves 8.

MEXICALI ANTELOPE MEAT LOAF

2 lbs. ground antelope
1 egg, slightly beaten
1/2 c. soft bread crumbs
1 tsp. salt
1 tsp. chili powder
1/8 tsp. pepper
1 can tomato sauce w/onions
1 can small red beans, drained
1 c. cheddar cheese, diced

Combine meat, egg, bread crumbs, salt, chili powder, and pepper. Add 1/2 c. tomato sauce and mix well. On waxed paper, form a 12" square. Press beans and cheese into meat to within 1/2" of edges. Roll up and pinch edges to seal. Bake at 375 degs. for 45 mins. Drain, spoon remaining sauce over top of meat. Bake 15 mins. longer. Let stand 10 mins. before cutting. Serves 8. Serve with coleslaw, corn bread or hot buttered tortillas or garlic bread, and baked peaches.

BIG HORN KABOBS

2-3 lbs. cubed meat
1 can condensed onion soup
1 c. dry red wine
salt and pepper
1/2 tsp. marjoram

Marinate meat 4-6 hrs. Drain, using favorite vegetable as first alternate on skewer and baste with sauce while cooking. Cook to doneness of individual taste.

SAVORY HERB WINE JERKY

1 1/2 lbs. top round
1 tsp. thyme leaves
2 cloves garlic, pressed
2 or 3 whole bay leaves
3/4 c. burgundy
1 tsp. salt
1/4 tsp. pepper
1 tsp. Worcestershire sauce

Trim and slice meat as for Mexican jerky. In a pan, combine garlic, burgundy, thyme, bay leaves, salt, Worcestershire sauce, and pepper. Simmer 5 mins. Transfer to bowl and cool. Add meat and marinate overnight. Dry as for Mexican jerky. Makes 5-6 ozs.

MACHACADO JERKY (BURRO)

2 cloves garlic, pressed
3/4 c. burgundy
1 tsp. thyme leaves
2 whole bay leaves
1 tsp. salt
1 tsp. Worcestershire sauce
1/4 tsp. pepper

Cut all fat from round and flank. Cut steak 1 1/2" thick then cut 1/2" thick by 1 1/2" wide and as long as possible. In stainless steel pan, combine garlic, burgundy, thyme, bay leaves, salt, Worcestershire sauce, and pepper. Simmer 5 mins. Transfer to bowl and cool. Add meat and marinate. Dry with paper towels. Makes 5-6 ozs.(dry in sun 4 days).

APPETIZER JERKY

5-6 lbs. lean round or flank steaks
   from big game
1 tsp. garlic powder
1 tsp. black pepper
1 T. seasoned salt
1/2 c. Worcestershire sauce
1 T. onion powder
1/2 c. soy sauce

Cut steaks 1 1/2" thick. Slice off strips 1/4" thick by 1 1/2" wide. Soak meat in seasoned salt, onion powder, black pepper, Worcestershire sauce, and soy sauce. Stir meat gently and let stand in refrigerator overnight. Drain and place meat on B.B.Q. grill so pieces do not touch. Use screening to keep out flies. Depending on weather, it will take from 3 to 4 days to dry. After second day, turn meat. When done, it will be dark and brittle and chewy. Store in covered container. Cheesecloth may be used to shield out insects.

BIG GAME S.O.S.

1 1/2-2 lbs. ground big game meat
1 med. onion, ground
1 green pepper, ground
1 large carrot, ground
2 T. flour
salt and pepper

Cook first 4 ingredients until meat is browned. Add flour and 2/3 c. water. Cook until thickened, stir constantly. Season to taste. Serve on toast or hot buttered biscuits, mashed potatoes, or rice. Hunter's breakfast.

CHINESE PEPPER STEAK
(ANY BIG GAME MEAT)

2 lbs. steak
2 T. water
1 1/3 c. bouillon
3 T. cornstarch
cooking oil
2 T. soy sauce
1 med. onion, coarsely chopped
2 tsp. sugar
1 green pepper, coarsely chopped
pinch ginger
1 stalk celery, coarsely chopped
1 16-oz. can Chinese vegetables

Partially thaw steaks, cut into thin strips, 1/8" slices. Brown in oil. Add bouillon, simmer 20 mins. Add onion, green pepper, and celery. Simmer 10 mins. Mix water and cornstarch, soy sauce, sugar, and ginger. Add to pan. Cook until slightly thick. Add drained vegetables. Serve with rice. Serves 6.

CARIBOU SCALLOPS

caribou steak
dash cayenne
salt and pepper
2 T. port wine
2 T. butter
1 T. currant jelly

Cut caribou steak about 1/2" thick and divide into portions 2" square. Season with salt and pepper, place in chafing dish, or covered fry pan with butter. Brown each side as quickly as possible. Add cayenne, wine, and jelly. Let simmer until inside shows only pink, then cut.

SPICY MEXICAN JERKY

1-1 1/2 lbs. boneless big game
  round, partially frozen
2 cloves garlic, pressed
1/8 tsp. cayenne
2 T. water
1 tsp. ground cumin
2 T. Worcestershire sauce
1 1/2 tsp. chili powder
1 tsp. salt

Trim and discard all fat from meat. Slice meat with the grain 1/8" thick and as long as possible with meat partially frozen. In a bowl, combine water, Worcestershire sauce, salt, garlic, cayenne, cumin, and chili powder. Stir to blend well. Add meat strips, mix thoroughly, cover, marinate several hrs. or overnight. Shake off any excess liquid and arrange strips close together (but not touching) on racks set in rimmed foil-lined 9" x 13" bake pans. Dry meat in 200 deg. oven for about 5-6 hrs. or until meat has turned black or dark brown and feels dry. Pat off any beads of oil. Cool, remove from racks and store in air-tight containers. Makes about 6 ozs.

CORNED BIG GAME

1 gal. hot water
1 1/2 lbs. pickling salt
1/2 lb. brown sugar
1 oz. baking soda
1 oz. cream of tartar
1 oz. pickling spice

Using stone crock or clean keg, dissolve all ingredients in hot water. When brine has cooled, pour enough of it over the boned and weighted meat to cover. After several weeks, you can cut off pieces as needed for table. Keep liquid over meat. This will do 25 lbs. or more game meat, boned and ready in roast-size chunks.

BIG GAME LIVER

1 lb. sliced liver
French dressing
2/3 c. seasoned flour
salt and pepper

Dip liver in French dressing, dredge in seasoned flour. Cook slowly in bacon drippings until brown on both sides. First night, first deer.

BIG GAME TONGUE

Cut tongue from elk, deer, moose, etc. Boil in salt water with onion and several dashes tabasco sauce about 3 hrs. until skin is loose and tender. Remove and skin. At this point, it may be thinly sliced for sandwiches or may be pickled.

BIG GAME HEART AND TONGUE

1 heart and tongue, cooked
1 1/2 c. cider vinegar
2/3 c. brown sugar
2 T. pickling spice
1 tsp. salt
1 tsp. pepper

Bring to a boil all ingredients but meat. Cut heart and tongue in strips 1/2" thick and about 3" long. Place in 1/2 gal. jars. Pour liquid mixture over all while still hot. Let cool and seal. Let sit about 1 week, add water as needed to cover. Left-over heart and tongue may be used the same way.

BIG GAME KIDNEYS - SAUTEED

Parboil kidneys, sauté in butter, about 4 mins. Use fork to stir meat around, season to taste, set aside. In drippings sauté 1 diced onion limp but not browned. Add 4 T. cooking dry sherry, cook until thickened. Sprinkle very lightly with cayenne pepper. Serve over kidneys.

OVEN-DRIED PIPIKAULA

1 1/2 lbs. flank, chuck, or rump
1/2 clove garlic, minced
1 T. salt
1/2 c. Kikoman soy sauce
dash pepper
1/2 tsp. sugar
1 tsp. minced ginger root
1 small red pepper, crushed

Trim all fat from game meat. Cut into strips 1/4" thick, 1 1/2" wide and as long as possible. Combine remaining ingredients. Mix with meat strips and pour into large plastic bag. Tie bag tightly and place in bowl in refrigerator. Let marinate 24 hrs. Preheat oven to 165 degs. and place meat on cooling racks set in baking sheets. Dry in oven 6-7 hrs. until of jerky texture. May be stored in freezer 6-8 months but should be used in about a week when refrigerated. Use as snack or heat through under broiler, then slice diagonally and serve as appetizer. Reduce salt to taste.

Notes

II

Small Game Tummy Fillers

JIM FANCY
RABBIT

JIM FANCY RABBIT

2 rabbits, cut up
1/4 c. coconut bits
2 c. pineapple juice
1/2 c. broken cashews
2 T. honey
2 slices crisp bacon, crumbled

Rub carcass with salt and red pepper. Marinate in a mixture of pineapple juice and honey for not less than 2 hrs. Fry bacon crisp, remove brown rabbit pieces in the drippings. Pour marinade over meat, cover. Simmer 2 1/2 hrs. or until meat is tender. Add coconut ruding last 45 mins. Garnish with cashews, bacon and pineapple chunks.

B.B.Q. RABBIT

Clean and wash the rabbit, a young plump one preferred. Open completely on the under side. Lay it flat with a small plate or saucer to keep it down in salted water, (clip off the rib cage if desired) for 1/2 hr. Wipe dry and broil whole when you have gashed it several times across the heavy part of the back, so the heat may penetrate. Your fire should be hot and clear, the rabbit turned often. When browned and tender, lay upon a very hot dish; season with pepper, salt and butter, preferably turning the rabbit over and over to soak up the melted butter. Cover and set in the oven 5 mins. Heat in a tin cup 2 tsp. of vinegar seasoned with 1 T. mustard. Anoint the rabbit with this. Cover and send to the table garnished with crisp parsley or water cress.

ROAST RABBIT

Empty the skin, and thoroughly wash the rabbit, wipe it dry, line the inside with sausage meat, and farce meat (bread crumbs well seasoned and worked up). Sew the stuffing inside, skewer back the head between the shoulders, cut it off. Cut off the fore parts of the shoulders and legs, bring them close to the body with a skewer to secure them. Wrap the rabbit in buttered paper. Keep it well basted, and a few mins. before it is done remove the paper and flour. Let it acquire a nice brown color. It should be done in 3/4 hr. Take out the skewers and serve with brown gravy and red currant jelly.

NORTHERN RABBIT STEW

2 young rabbits, cut up
1/4 c. parsley, chopped
1/4 c. oil and drippings
1 onion, sliced
4 c. boiling water
2 tsp. salt
1/4 tsp. pepper
1/2 c. celery, sliced
1/4 c. flour
3 med. potatoes, diced
1/2 c. cold water
3 med. carrots, diced

Brown rabbits in oil in Dutch oven, add 4 c. boiling water, cover and simmer about 1 hr., depending on the age of the rabbits. Add vegetables and seasoning, cook until vegetables are tender, about 20-25 mins. Combine flour and cold water to form a paste, add to stew. Stir until slightly thickened. Dumplings go good with this stew.

TRAIL FRIED RABBIT

Skin, clean rabbit, wash, cut up. Salt each piece, shake in seasoned flour. Fry in skillet or deep fat 50 mins. Same for squirrel.

LIMA BEAN RABBIT STEW

2 c. dried lima beans
1 bay leaf
1 rabbit, cut in serving pieces
1 med. onion, diced
1 1/2 qts. cold water
small bunch carrots, sliced
2 tsp. salt
2 green peppers, chopped
1/8 tsp. pepper
2 stalks celery, diced
1 tsp. monosodium glutamate
2 T. butter

Soak beans in water overnight. Place rabbit in boiling water with drained beans. Add salt, pepper, monosodium glutamate, bay leaf, onion, and carrots. Simmer 1 hr. Add water as desired. Add peppers and celery last 15 mins. of cooking time with butter. Thicken gravy if desired.

FRICASSEED RABBIT

The best way of cooking rabbits is believed to be fricasseeing them. Cut them up or disjoint them. Put them into a stew pan; season them with cayenne pepper, salt and chopped parsley. Pour in 1 pt. of warm water or veal broth if you have it. Stew over a slow fire until the rabbits are quite tender, adding (when they are about half done), some bits of butter rolled in flour. Just before you take it from the fire, enrich the gravy with a gill of more thick cream, with some nutmeg grated into it. Stir the gravy well, take care it does not boil causing the cream to curdle. Put the pieces of rabbit on a hot dish and pour the gravy over them.

REAL GERMAN HASENPFEFFER

1 young 3 lb. rabbit, cut up
1/4 tsp. pepper
1 1/2 c. cold water
2 tsp. sugar 1 1/2 c. cider vinegar
1/8 tsp. allspice
1 tsp. whole cloves
1 med. onion, sliced
3 bay leaves
1/2 c. flour
2 tsp. salt
butter or shortening

Combine vinegar, water, spices, seasonings and onions. Marinate rabbit pieces in covered crock or china bowl at least 12 hrs., 1 or 2 days would be better. Remove rabbit and drain. Coat pieces in seasoned flour. Brown well in 1/4" of shortening in heavy skillet. Remove excess fat and add marinate fluid. Cover and simmer 1 or 2 hrs. according to how tough the rabbit is. Remove rabbit to hot platter, thicken liquid for gravy with flour or finely crumbled ginger snaps. Serves 6.

PACK TRAIN RABBIT PIE

Soak rabbits in salted water, drain. Parboil meat with onion chopped, chunk of bacon, 1 large diced carrot. Place all in Dutch oven, cover, cook until meat is tender. Remove meat, thicken gravy with 2 T. flour to 1 c. liquid. Return rabbits. Using a bisquit mix (about 1 c. of mix according to the directions), pat into a cover for the stew, about 1/4" thick; cut 2-3 slices in dough. Place over contents in oven and cook over hot coals, about 25-30 mins. Place coals on lid.

BAKED RABBIT

Proceed as for roast rabbit. In a good oven it will take about the same time as roasting. Most cooks garnish the rabbit with slices of lemon and serve up with currant jelly. Cut head off before sending to table, but it remains a matter of individual taste.

RABBIT SOUP

Dissect the rabbit, crack the bones, and prepare as venison soup except use 3 small onions instead of 1. In granite ware place a bunch of sweet herbs and peppers. A pt. of tomatoes may also be used.

STUFFED RACCOON

1 apple, diced
2 pkgs. country style poultry dressing
1 stalk celery, diced
1 stick margarine
3/4 c. walnuts, chopped

Remove all fat from coon and wash meat thoroughly, salt cavity. Mix all ingredients but meat together lightly. Stuff cavity and skewer or sew cavity closed. Roast 3 hrs. or until tender at 350 degs. Serve with tangy beans, tart salad, and hot sour dough biscuits.

PIONEER RACCOON

Remove all fat, rub well with salt and pepper, wrap in foil and roast 3-4 hrs. at 325 degs. Remove foil for last 30 mins. Baste frequently with drippings, add water as needed. Dust with flour for a crisp crust, rub meat with garlic, onion, or sage to cut down on gamey taste. Add 1 c. red wine and thicken drippings for gravy.

BAKED ARMADILLO

1 dressed armadillo
salt and pepper
1/2 c. butter

Rub armadillo with salt and pepper. Cover with butter. Wrap in heavy-duty foil and grill or bake in oven. Armadillo most closely resembles pork, so cooking time should be the same as for fresh pork roast of the same weight. When done, remove foil, add more butter and brown.

SWEET AND SOUR ARMADILLO

Use same cooking method as for fried armadillo. Prepare sweet and sour sauce of your choice. Serve over hot buttered noodles or rice with tossed salad.

B.B.Q. ARMADILLO

1 armadillo, cleaned
1/2 c. butter
salt and pepper
B.B.Q. sauce of your choice

Season and cook according to baking instructions. After removing foil, baste with your B.B.Q. sauce.

FRIED ARMADILLO

1 dressed armadillo
butter
seasoned flour

Cut armadillo into serving pieces. Dredge in seasoned flour. Fry in butter until brown and tender. Make a cream gravy to serve with the meat. Serve with hot noodles or buttered rice.

DRESSING AN ARMADILLO

Using a sharp knife, cut the meat on the underside of the tail and head away from the shell as far as can be reached. Pull the head away from the shell and simultaneously cut the meat from the shell. The carcass should come away from the shell cleanly. Use shears to cut off head and feet. Cut through belly muscle and use shears to cut through pelvic and breast bones. Holding carcass by tail, cut or pull out entrails, remove all sweat glands and feet, cut off tail. Wash and cook your favorite way. Resembles pork.

MT. GOAT RACK-O-RIBS

Make a 3 ft. fire bed with plenty of hardwood coals. Make racks uniform in thickness. Stand ribs on green stakes before fire bed (as for planked fish). Baste meat, reverse rack occasionally for even roasting. Cook about 2 hrs. Cut into desirable sections for eating, when done; let each diner season his own.

DESERT CHICKEN COCKTAIL

1/2 c. celery, chopped
1/8 tsp. pepper
pinch of thyme
2 T. salad dressing
1/4 tsp. celery salt

Clean and dress rattler. Bury head. Parboil in salt water until meat can be stripped from the bone, chop meat fine. Add finely chopped celery. Season with thyme, celery salt, and pepper. Add salad dressing, toss lightly. Serve on lettuce leaves. Delete lettuce and make paté. Serve on toast or cocktail crackers, brown lightly in broiler.

SMOKED DESERT CHICKEN

5-6" sections of cleaned and dressed snakes, marinate 24 hrs. in heavy salt brine. Drain, rinse, and brush sections with bacon grease. Broil about 10 mins. per side. Place in smoker, smoke 4 hrs. with soaked hardwood chips. Broil tender or leave in smoker 1 hr. longer.

WOODCHUCK POT ROAST

Dredge up (cut up pieces of a young woodchuck) in seasoned flour, use your favorite seasoning, brown in hot fat. In a preheated Dutch oven, add 1 c. boiling water, 3 T. lime or lemon juice, simmer 3 or 4 hrs. or until tender. Just before serving pour in 1/2 c. of red or sherry wine.

CUT ON DOTTED LINE

FRIED RATTLESNAKE

rattlesnake
buttermilk
salt and pepper
pancake mix

Cut meat in 2" chunks. Soak meat in salt and buttermilk 1 hr. Drain, dredge in pancake mix and fry 7 mins. in deep, hot fat. Drain well. Serve with wilted salad and potato cakes.

JACKRABBIT JERKY (No. 1)

In camp, cut meat into thin strips, salt and pepper to taste. Start drying process on grill over hot coals for a few minutes, then lay in sun until right dryness is achieved. At home, oven dry at 160 degs. Use standard recipes.

JACKRABBIT JERKY (No. 2)

rabbit
2 whole bay leaves
2 cloves garlic, pressed
1 tsp. of salt
3/4 c. red wine
1 tsp. Worcestershire sauce
1 tsp. thyme leaves
1/4 tsp. pepper

Cut skinned and cleaned rabbit. Marinate in garlic. Simmer 5 mins. to blend. Transfer to bowl, cool. Add meat and marinate 5 hrs. Arrange on cake racks in baking sheets, do not overlap. Screen out flies. Keep in direct sun, cover at night. After 2 days, turn. Dry 2 days longer.

DESERT CHICKEN JERKY

Clean and skin snake (bury rattlesnake head).
Cut snake in 5-6" pieces, marinate sections for
24 hrs. in heavy salt brine. Drain, rinse,
brush sections with bacon grease. Bull snake
is a good substitute for rattler. Dry over
slow, smoky hardwood fire until nearly crisp.
Smoke and dry until tough to chew. May be
wrapped in foil and carried almost indefinitely.

FIVE-SPICE PORK JERKY

**1 1/2 lbs. boneless javelina or pork
   loin, partially frozen
1/4 tsp. Chinese 5-spice seasoning
1 T. sherry
2 T. packed brown sugar
1 tsp. salt
3 T. soy sauce
1/3 c. water
1/4 tsp. pepper**

Trim fat and slice pork as for Mexican jerky.
In bowl, combine brown sugar, soy sauce,
sherry, salt, water, pepper, and Chinese five-
spice seasoning. Add 2 garlic cloves, pressed.
Add pork, marinate and dry as for Mexican
jerky. Makes 7 ozs.

SADDLE OF JAVELINA

Season saddle of javelina with salt and pepper,
sprinkle lightly with thyme. Roast uncovered
at 325 degs. for 35 mins. per lb. Baste
frequently with drippings. Thicken drippings
for gravy if desired. Serve with mashed yams
and hot apple sauce.

ROAST JAVELINA WITH SAGE ONIONS

3 lbs. loin roast
salt and pepper
8 med. onions
3/4 tsp. rubbed sage
3 T. bacon drippings

Place roast in shallow pan, rub with salt and pepper, roast at 325 degs. for 2-2 1/2 hrs. Peel onions, cut into sixths, sprinkle with sage, sauté in drippings until brown. Season with salt and pepper. Carve pork, serve with onions.

JAVELINA B.B.Q.

5-6 lbs. meat, ham, shoulder
1/2 c. drippings or broth
4-oz. can tomato sauce
1 med. onion, diced
1/4 tsp. garlic salt
3 T. brown sugar
1/4 tsp. dry mustard
1/8 c. lemon juice
1/8 c. vinegar
1/4 c. hot catsup

Cook meat until well done. Mix all other ingredients and pour over meat. Simmer about 15 mins. longer, blend well. Serve on sandwich rolls. Serves 8-10. Bear or burro may be substituted.

ROAST YOUNG JAVELINA

Skin out and clean pig. Be sure to remove musk glands on the back. Split the pig on a green pale (not resinous) over a good bed of hardwood coals. Roast your porker. Use your favorite B.B.Q. sauce to baste. This is real eating!

SAUERKRAUT AND JAVELINA RIBS

1 lb. ham hocks
2 ribs celery, 3" chunks
3 lbs. javelina spareribs (country
   style)
1 tart apple, halved
1 large onion, halved
seasoning to taste

Place ribs on roaster and place in 400 deg. oven for 45 mins. uncovered. Remove, pour off all but 2 T. of drippings, save. Place 2 #2 cans sauerkraut around roasting meat. Place ham hocks and rest of ingredients around meal, return to oven and reduce heat to 375 degs. for 1 hr. 15 mins. Serve with spicy applesauce, coleslaw, hot biscuits.

POSSUM PIE

1/2 c. vinegar
2 carrots, sliced thin
1 large onion, diced
2 stalks celery, diced

Remove all fat from possum. Parboil with ingredients. Cook until meat can be removed from bone, remove and dice. Using a double crust 9" pie shell, fill with drained meat and vegetables. Bake until crust is brown. Thicken liquor or gravy. Serve with cooked greens, hot corn bread, and mashed yams.

BAKED POSSUM (No. 1)

1 possum
1 c. herb stuffing
1/2 c. celery, chopped
1 med. onion, chopped
1/4 c. chopped walnuts
1/4 c. pecans, chopped
1/2 c. butter, melted
salt and pepper
3 T. water
1/2 tsp. poultry seasoning

Clean possum and remove excess fat. Mix all ingredients but meat. Blend well and fill cavity, sew or skewer shut. Place meat in Dutch oven or roast. Bake at 400 degs., covered for 1 hr. Remove cover and brown to finish. Serves 4. Serve with buttered mashed yams, cooked greens, hot biscuits, and coleslaw.

BAKED POSSUM (No. 2)

Prepare possum for cooking, remove glands from legs and back. Simmer in salted water until tender, remove. Wipe dry, season with pepper. Place in shallow roasting pan. Surround with parboiled sweet potatoes. Bake in 350 deg. oven until a rich golden brown. Baste every 10 mins. with drippings from broth.

BROILED POSSUM

Split a skinned cleaned possum. Rub with salt and pepper and small amount of sage. Broil over hot coals about 1 hr. or until tender. Turn and baste with fresh lemon juice frequently while watching your coals.

OPOSSUM AND SASSAFRAS

Prepare possum as for roasting. Rub with salt and pepper. Stick fresh green sassafras twigs thickly in meat. Roast unstuffed until tender about 1 1/2 hrs. in 300 deg. oven (1/2 hr. per pound).

ROAST BEAVER

Remove all fat from young beaver. In large pan, cook meat in 1 qt. water, 1 tsp. soda. Parboil about 10 mins. Drain, place carcass in roaster, sprinkle with salt and pepper. Cover with strips of bacon and sliced onion. Roast at 350 degs. until meat falls away from bones. Add water as needed.

BEAVER TAIL SOUP

1 1/2 tsp. salt
3 carrots, sliced
2 med. onions, sliced
1/4 tsp. pepper
1 clove garlic, minced
5 stalks celery, chunked
2 c. egg noodles
1 small can peas, drained

Skin and remove fat from tails, cut into small pieces and soak about 8 hrs. in water to cover with 1 c. vinegar, 2 T. salt for each qt. of water. Drain and place in large kettle with 4 qts. boiling water, salt, onions, garlic, carrots, pepper, and celery. When meat is almost done, add egg noodles and peas. Serves 6.

BEAVER

Remove kernels in small of back and front armpits between ribs and shoulder. Hang in cold several days. Poach in salted water for 1 hr. Braise as beef until tender. **Beaver tail:** hold over open flame until rough skin blisters, remove from heat. When cool, peel off skin. Roast over coals or simmer until tender.

BEAVER PREPARATION

Back in pioneer days, beaver was a delicacy looked forward to with delight. Beaver tail was then and is now a true gourmet item. Beaver meat is dark red and rich. It is tender and delicious, much like roast pork. A mature beaver may weigh up to 60 lbs. Younger animals make better eating. Remove all fat before attempting to cook a beaver. A good overnight soaking in vinegar salt brine is suggested.

PAN FRIED MUSQUASH (MUSKRAT)

**1 musquash in quarters
1/2 c. flour
vinegar brine
4 T. vegetable oil
salt and pepper**

Wash carcass well, quarter, soak overnight in vinegar brine, and rinse in cold water. Dry thoroughly, sprinkle with salt and pepper, dust with flour, fry in hot oil. Brown on all sides, reduce heat and cook slowly 1 hr. Add small amount of oil if necessary during cooking time to keep from sticking. When tender, remove to heated platter. Use 3 T. pan drippings to make gravy, add 3 T. flour and cook, stirring constantly until bubbly. Add 1 1/2 c. of milk and continue cooking until gravy thickens. Season to taste with salt and pepper, serve gravy over musquash.

B.B.Q. MUSQUASH

1 cleaned musquash
3 T. oil or drippings
salt and pepper
Bear B.B.Q. sauce or your choice of
   sauce
1/2 c. flour

Wash carcass well, cut into serving pieces. Soak overnight in vinegar brine, rinse in cold water. Dry thoroughly. Lightly sprinkle with salt and pepper, shake in flour, brown in oil in heavy skillet until browned on all sides. Cover and cook over low heat until tender. Cut bacon up and simmer with onions in 1 1/2 c. water. Remove meat from pan, and strain onion water into pan drippings. Simmer until most of water has evaporated. Stir 1 c. evaporated milk, season to taste. Add 1 1/2 T. brandy, simmer 5 mins. Pour sauce over meat and serve.

ROAST SKUNK (ARGENTINE DELICACY)

Clean and skin skunk. Be careful fur does not touch meat, do not rupture scent glands. Remove all fat, soak 8 hrs. in water, vinegar, and salt. Remove and parboil about 35 mins. Remove and dry, season with salt and pepper. Place in roaster and bake at 375 degs. about 1 1/2 hrs. or until tender. Parboil with 2 small onions and tops of 2 stalks of celery.

BAKED COON OR POSSUM

Prepare whole carcass; rub well with salt and pepper, be sure to remove all fat. For stuffing, use 12-14 slices toast, cubed; 1 tsp. stick margarine; 1 1/2 tsp. poultry seasoning; 1 small onion, diced; 1 tsp. salt; 1/4 tsp. pepper; and hot water to moisten. Mix all together. Pack into cavity, roast at 375 degs. for 2-3 hrs. until tender.

PICKLED MUSKRAT AND DUMPLINGS

    1 c. water
    1 T. salt
    1 c. cider
    1 T. pickling spice
    1 bay leaf

Place cleaned carcass in solution. Let stand in cool place 48 hrs. Then simmer in marinade until tender. Remove meat, strain off spices and bay leaf. Thicken to desired consistency. This is best served with **POTATO DUMPLINGS**:

    1 med. onion, sliced
    2 eggs
    2 T. bacon grease
    1/2 c. flour
    4 c. diced bread
    salt
    1 c. mashed potatoes

Fry onion in bacon grease. Pour over bread, mix by hand. Add potatoes, mix thoroughly. Add eggs, flour, and salt to taste. Lightly fashion into large balls, drop into boiling water in uncovered kettle for 20 mins. Serve with brown gravy.

SOUTHERN FRIED MUSKRAT

salt and pepper
2 eggs
flour
1/2 c. milk
cornmeal
1 1/2 c. milk

Wash muskrat, cut in quarters, soak 1 hr. or more in salted water, and rinse. Dry with cloth. Sprinkle with salt and pepper. Beat eggs with 1/2 c. milk. Dip pieces in mixture then in cornmeal. Brown all sides in hot fat, reduce heat, cook slowly 1 hr. Remove meat, pour off all but 3 T. fat. Add 3 T. flour, stirring rapidly. Slowly add 1 1/2 c. milk and cook until thickened. Season to taste. Serve gravy over meat. Serve with mashed sweet potatoes, mustard greens, a crusty bread, apple, walnut, and celery salad. Makes real eating.

B.B.Q. MUSKRAT

Skin and clean 2 young rats, rinse, dry, cut into serving pieces. Brown pieces on all sides in hot grease. Place in Dutch oven, cover with B.B.Q. sauce. Bake at 350 degs. 1 hr. or until tender, baste frequently with pan drippings.

BAKED MUSKRAT

1 onion, sliced
1/4 c. vinegar
6-8 slices bacon
1/4 c. water

Using only hams and shoulders, parboil with onion about 30 mins. Drain, shake pieces in seasoned flour, place in Dutch oven or roaster. Cover with bacon. Add vinegar, water. Bake in preheated oven, 375 degs., until tender. Baste frequently with drippings. Serve with mashed yams, mustard or turnip greens, Waldorf walnut, apple salad, and hot corn bread.

FRIED PORCUPINE LIVER

The liver in a porky is quite large. Slice liver in 1/2" slices, remove tubes and the membranes. Fry in margarine about 1 min. per side. Remove to hot platter, add 1/2 c. claret wine to pan juices, boil rapidly. Pour over meat slices. Bacon grease may be used in place of margarine.

PORCUPINE STEW

porky meat cut in cubes
1/2 c. diced celery
1 large onion
3 c. diced turnips
2 tsp. salt
1/4 tsp. pepper
1/2 c. sliced onions
1/4 tsp. basil
2 T. melted butter
1 T. flour
1 green pepper, chopped
8-oz. can tomato sauce

Parboil meat 45 mins. with sliced onion and salt. Drain. Sauté onions in butter until clear. Add meat which has been dredged in flour. Add 1 qt. water, vegetables, and seasonings. Cook until tender, thicken slightly with left-over dredging flour dissolved in water.

ROAST PORCUPINE

Clean out entrails and be careful of spines. In clean cavity, place heart and 2 small onions. Save liver for later. Tie cavity shut. Plaster thickly with mud. Cook in open fire about 2 1/2 hrs. Crack off hardened mud, spines will adhere to it. May taste of evergreen depending what the animal has been feeding on.

LYNX AND WILD RICE

2 c. wild rice
salt and pepper
boiled lynx, cubed
Parmesan cheese
1 c. heavy cream

Spread wild rice or wild mix on bottom of baking pan with boiled cubed lynx meat and cream. Season with salt and pepper (over top of rice). Sprinkle with Parmesan cheese (paprika optional). Place in preheated oven, 350 degs., until a nice tan crust forms.

WOODCHUCK PATTIES

Clean woodchuck, remove glands from under forelegs and at small of back. Remove meat from bones and grind. Add bread crumbs, onion, salt and pepper, egg, and bacon drippings. Mix thoroughly, form into patties. Dip into egg then bread crumbs, fry until brown in hot fat. Cover with currant jelly sauce and bake in slow oven 1 hr.

FRICASSEED WHISTLE PIG

Clean woodchuck, remove all fat and glands, cut into pieces. Rub with salt and pepper, roll in flour, and fry in hot fat until brown. Add 2 c. water, cover, simmer 2 hrs. or until tender.

SQUIRREL POT PIE

2 or more squirrels
1 qt. water
1 tsp. lemon juice
1 tsp. salt
1 chicken bouillon cube
1/4 c. water
1 tsp. Worcestershire sauce
1 med. onion, diced
1 c. biscuit mix

Cut squirrels into serving pieces, shake in seasoned flour, save flour for thickening. Brown meat in oil or bacon drippings. Place in Dutch oven and add all remaining ingredients but onion and biscuit mix. Sauté onion in drippings and place with meat. Cover oven and simmer 1 hr. Mix and roll out biscuit mix, cut and place on top of meat. Place lid on for 10 mins. Then take lid off for 10 mins. Make gravy.

ABERT SQUIRREL AND RED WINE

Use 2 good-sized squirrels, cleaned and cut into serving pieces. Sauté pieces in bacon drippings. Dice and sauté 6 thick bacon strips for drippings. Add thyme, garlic, and tomato paste. Dip meat in seasoned flour before sautéing. Cover meat with red wine and chicken broth. Cook until tender, set aside. Sauté sliced fresh mushrooms. Serve with squirrel on toast or good bannock hot cakes.

III

Winged Creatures

PHEASANT
HAWAIIAN

PHEASANT HAWAIIAN

Prepare large squares of heavy duty foil, pheasant breasts (1 per serving). Season breasts. Place on foil with pineapple slice, 1/2 tomato (2 wedges), and potato slices. Add 1 T. pineapple juice. Wrap in foil, place in coals. Turn several times; about 40-50 mins.

CRANBERRY-STUFFED QUAIL
(CORNISH HENS)

2/3 c. cranberries, chopped
3 c. toasted raisin bread cubes
2 T. sugar
4 T. butter
1 tsp. orange peel, shredded
4 tsp. orange juice
1/2 tsp. salt
4-5 quail (4 Cornish hens)
1/8 tsp. cinnamon
salt
cooking oil
1/4 c. orange juice

In bowl, combine sugar, cranberries, orange peel, salt, and cinnamon. Add bread cubes, sprinkle with half of the melted butter, and 4 tsp. orange juice. Toss lightly. Season cavities of bird with salt and pepper, lightly stuff birds with mixture. Place breast side up on rack in shallow pan. Brush with oil or margarine, cover loosely with foil. Roast at 375 degs. for 30 mins. Combine orange juice and remaining melted butter, uncover and baste birds with mixture. Return to oven. Roast uncovered until well done about 1 hr. longer, basting twice with orange juice and butter mixture. Serves 4.

FOIL ROASTED DUCK

1 duck
salt and pepper
1 whole med. onion
1/4 c. red wine
1/2 tsp. thyme
1 T. margarine

Rub inside of bird with salt and pepper. Place whole onion inside bird. Place on a large sheet of foil. Sprinkle thyme on duck and place margarine on breast. Wrap loosely and bake at 325 degs. for 3 1/2 hrs. Serve with wild rice. Wrap buttered slices of French bread in foil. Bake 10 mins. Serve with three-bean salad and cherry pie.

ROAST DUCKS

Wash and dry cleaned ducks carefully; make a dressing of sage, onions and stale bread crumbs. Insert and sew up carefully that the dressing may not escape. If tender, ducks do not require more than 1 hr. to roast. Keep them well basted, and a few mins. before serving, dredge lightly with flour to make them plump. Send to the table hot, with a good brown gravy poured over them, accompany with currant jelly and peas if in season.

TO ROAST SNIPER, WOODCOCK, PALVERS

Pick (pluck) and clean these birds immediately. Wipe dry, season them just slightly with salt and pepper. Cut as many slices of bread as you have birds. Toast them brown, butter them, lay them in the pan, dredge the birds in flour, and put them in the oven with a brisk fire. Baste them with fresh butter. They will be done in 20-30 mins. Serve them up laid on the toast, garnish with sliced oranges or orange jelly.

SAUSAGE-STUFFED DUCK

1 oven-ready duck
2 c. sausage
4 T. margarine
salt and pepper
2 c. stuffing mix
1/2 c. canned milk
1 T. onion, minced

Soak stuffing mix, press dry. Rub inside of bird with salt and pepper. Loosely fill cavity with stuffing. In roaster, place bird breast up for roasting. Wrap wings with bacon slices to keep from drying out. Roast uncovered at 350 degs. about 25 mins. per lb.

SIMMERED CROW

Scald and pluck birds, remove oil glands above tail, split in half and clean. Soak overnight in salt and vinegar solution with small amount of soda. Dredge in seasoned flour, brown in margarine, add 1/4 c. water and 1 sliced onion. Cover and simmer over low heat until tender.

GAME BIRD SALAD

2 1/2 c. left-over game bird, diced
2 T. soy sauce
1/3 c. diced celery
2/3 c. mayonnaise or salad dressing
1/3 c. water chestnuts, diced

Makes 3 cups. Use as sandwich filling or serve on lettuce leaf.

WOODCOCK OR QUAIL PIMENTO

6 woodcock or quail
3 green peppers, minced
1/2 c. flour
1/2 c. cooking sherry
1/2 c. cooking oil
3 pimentos, minced
6 small onions
2 c. chicken bouillon
1 clove garlic, crushed (opt.)
salt and pepper
1/8 tsp. saffron

Cut birds into quarters, dredge in seasoned flour. Heat oil in skillet, add onion, garlic, and meat. Turn meat often to brown evenly. When browned, place in deep casserole. Add saffron, pepper, sherry, pimentos, and stock. Cover. Cook at 450 degs. for 15 mins. Serve with wild rice mix.

GRILLED WOODCOCK

8 woodcock, plucked
10 peppercorns
1 c. dry red wine
1/4 tsp. fennel seed
3 T. lemon juice
butter
4 T. onion, minced
bread crumbs
3 bay leaves, broken

Mix marinade of wine, lemon juice, onions, bay leaves, peppercorns, and fennel seed. Marinate woodcock in this mixture for 3 hrs., turning often. Just before broiling, remove birds, roll in fine bread crumbs, coating well. Grease a piece of foil with melted butter, place in broiler pan. Dot birds with butter. Place on foil. Broil 4" above coals, 4 mins. per side (total time 8 mins.). Serve on heated plate with sauce made half-and-half of melted butter and black raspberry jam. Serves 4.

RARE ROASTED TIMBERDOODLE
(WOODCOCK)

8 woodcock, plucked
3 T. butter
1 cooking apple
1/2 c. port wine

Preheat oven to 450 degs. Place slice of apple
in each bird with butter. Place in roasting
pan. Pour a little port over each bird, roast
25 mins. Baste with pan juices several times.
Serves 4.

QUAIL ON TRENCHERS

4 quail
6 mushrooms
1/2 c. melted butter
2 T. parsley, chopped
1/2 c. water

Clean and pluck quail. Sprinkle inside and out
with salt and pepper and flour. In skillet,
melt butter. Add quail, brown all sides. Add
water and mushrooms. Cover, cook about 10 mins.
Add parsley. Cover, cook 10 mins. longer. Serve
on trenchers with pan sauce. Serves 4.

GLAZED ROASTED QUAIL

6 ready quail
salt and pepper
nut stuffing
1 c. chicken bouillon
1/2 c. margarine, melted
2 T. cornstarch

Stuff quail, place in shallow roaster. Pour
butter over birds, season with salt and pepper.
Roast in oven at 425 degs. for 1 hr., baste
frequently. Glaze with bouillon when done. Mix
bouillon with a little water.

QUAIL - CORNISH HENS (HAWAII)

2 Cornish hens or 4 quail, split
1/4 c. coconut bits
2 c. sherry and water
1/2 c. crushed almonds
2 T. honey
4 slices crisp bacon, crumbled

Split birds, rinse, wipe dry, season with salt and red pepper sprinkled on. Marinate in wine, water and honey for 2 hrs. Fry bacon, remove, brown bird halves in drippings. Pour marinade over meat, cover, simmer 1-1 1/2 hrs. or until tender. Add bacon, coconut and mandarin orange segments as garnish. Serve on hot buttered noodles with cold white wine. 4 portions.

BROILED QUAIL

2 quail, split
salt and pepper
1 tsp. marjoram
2 T. margarine

Rub halves of quail with salt and pepper and marjoram. Let stand 1 hr. Put skin side down in preheated Dutch oven, brush with melted margarine. Bake about 20 mins. Turn and brush again with melted margarine. Finish baking until tender.

QUAIL AND WILD RICE

Brown birds in oil, add salt and pepper, some chopped ham, cognac, and 1 c. chicken bouillon. Let simmer until tender. Remove meat, add bouillon and cook rice in it. Serve quail on rice.

BANDTAIL OR QUAIL

1/2 c. celery, chopped
1 pkg. spaghetti sauce mix
1/2 c. onion, chopped
1 can tomato sauce

Pluck and clean birds, split birds, brown in bacon grease or margarine, season with salt and pepper and cayenne. Place in covered pan, simmer 1/2 hr. Add chopped celery, onion, spaghetti sauce mix, and tomato sauce. Simmer 1/2 hr. more. Serve with spaghetti, tossed salad, sour dough biscuits. Also good with other game birds.

QUAIL TRENCHERS

Select hard or soft rolls slightly larger than quail. Cut in half lengthwise, scoop out center forming cup for bird. Butter and toast slightly. Place bird in cup, use favorite sauce over bird. Good with applesauce.

CHRISTMAS GOOSE

1 dressed goose, thawed
1 lemon, halved
1 T. salt
apple
giblets and neck for broth
prune stuffing
1/2 tsp. pepper

Remove excess fat from body cavity, render, save, refrigerate for later. Rub inside and out with lemon, salt, and pepper. Loosely stuff neck cavity. Fasten neck to back with skewer, put remaining stuffing in body cavity. Place wings behind back, tie legs together or tuck in skin. Place goose breast side up on rack in large roaster. Prick breast skin to allow fat to drain off. Roast at 325 degs. for 4 1/2-5 hrs. or until meaty parts of legs feel soft when pressed between fingers and juices run beige rather than pink when pinched. Spoon off fat several times during roasting. Remove goose to carving board, or platter, keep warm. Let stand 30 mins. before carving. **Gravy:** put 4 T. butter in heavy skillet, broth from parts, cook down, add 1/2 c. chopped giblets and neck. Add 1 T. red currant jelly to taste and 2 T. sherry wine. Season, thicken if necessary.

ROAST GOOSE

1 goose, drawn and cleaned
salt, pepper to taste
1/4 c. cooking oil
3 scallions
1 clove garlic, peeled
glaze for goose
1 6-oz. can orange concentrate,
   thawed
2 T. honey
1/4 c. soy sauce
2 T. orange marmalade
1/4 c. dry sherry
1 tsp. fresh ginger, minced

Wipe goose with oil inside and out (cut off gobs of fat, save). Bruise garlic and rub goose inside and out. Discard garlic; season with salt and pepper. Place whole scallions in bird cavity to absorb grease. Using a large mixing bowl place all glaze ingredients in it. Stir well to blend. Place bird in roasting pan, spoon glaze over bird (breast up), 450 deg. oven until done; continue for another 45 mins., basting every 10 mins. Skin will be golden brown. Discard scallions before serving.

GOOSE GREASE

Save and render out the heavy fat from geese. A wonderful base for ointments, etc. None better.

CANADA GOOSE

**1 10-12 lb. goose
1 lemon
salt and pepper
1 1/2 c. prunes, chopped
1 1/2 c. cranberries
1 1/2 c. celery, chopped
1 1/2 c. apple, diced
1/2 tsp. salt**

Remove excess fat from bird and rub bird inside and out with cut lemon and salt and pepper. Mix ingredients and lightly stuff bird, sew opening shut. Truss bird and place breast down on rack in roaster. Roast at 325 degs. about 4 1/2 hrs. or until drumstick meat feels soft. After 3 hrs., turn bird over. Remove fat as it accumulates (save it). Use grease seasoned with apple and onion to fry potatoes, grease may also be used for biscuits or hot breads. To make seasoned shortening, let cool and rinse. Place in saucepan with 1 apple cut in wedges and 1 small onion cut in sixths. Cook until all water evaporates (over low heat). Strain into container, chill.

PHEASANT IN SOUR CREAM

1 pheasant, quartered
1 4-oz. can mushrooms
1 10-oz. can cream of mushroom soup
1/4 c. grated Parmesan cheese
1/4 c. onion, chopped
1/2 c. sour cream

Place meat in pan in single layer, skin side up. In bowl, blend soup, mushrooms, cheese, and onion. Spread over meat. Bake at 350 degs. for 1 1/2-2 hrs. or until tender. Baste with sauce.

PHEASANT BAKED IN WINE

6 T. tomato paste
3/4 c. white port wine
6 T. tomato sauce

Cut bird or birds into serving pieces, rub with salt and pepper, dredge in seasoned flour, brown in margarine. Sprinkle with onion and garlic salt. Remove to baking pan 13" x 9". In bowl, combine tomato paste, tomato sauce, and wine. Pour over meat and bake at 250 degs. for 2 hrs. For large bird or more than 1, add 1/2 hr. baking time.

PHEASANT YORKSHIRE STYLE

2 c. cooked diced pheasants
1/4 tsp. baking powder
2 T. melted butter
1/2 tsp. salt
1 c. flour
1 c. milk
2 eggs

Place pheasant in greased baking dish, brush with butter. Combine eggs and milk. Mix with dry ingredients, beating until smooth (batter will be thin). Pour batter over pheasant, bake at 350 degs. for 30 mins. Serve with left-over chicken gravy or cream of chicken soup.

PHEASANT AND BISCUITS

For your game supper your contribution should amount to:

**45 lbs. pheasant (4 fat stewing
   hens)
5 stalks celery with leaves (chunks)
1/3 c. salt
1 1/2 lbs. cooked peas
1 tsp. black pepper
2 lbs. fresh cooked, diced carrots
2 onions, quartered**

Cover pheasant with cold water and cook with salt, pepper, onions, celery, until tender. Remove meat from bones, cut into 1" pieces, strain broth, make gravy, add cooked peas and carrots. Serve hot over or with hot biscuits.

JELLIED PHEASANT

Cook 6 pheasants in small quantity of water until the meat will part from the bone easily. Season to taste with salt and pepper. Just as soon as cool enough to handle, remove bones and skin; place meat in deep pan or mold just as it comes off the bone using gizzard, liver and heart until mold is nearly full. To the water left in the kettle add 3/4 box clear gelatin (Knox) (some add juice of a lemon) dissolved in a little warm water, and boil until it is reduced to a little less than a qt. Pour over the chicken in the mold, leave to cool, slice with a very sharp knife and serve. The slices will not easily break up if directions are followed. Rabbit is also good fixed this way, same ingredients and measurements.

PHEASANT STEWED IN CREAM

1 dressed pheasant
1/2 c. seasoned flour
2 T. melted butter
1 pt. cream
1/2 c. celery, chopped
1 small onion, minced
1 T. flour
1 4-oz. can chopped mushrooms

Disjoint bird and dredge in seasoned flour. Brown quickly in butter. Use heavy skillet or Dutch oven. Add cream, celery, and onion. Simmer until tender. Thicken pan juices for gravy, use flour in a little water, add mushrooms.

SMOTHERED DOVES

12 doves, cleaned, plucked, washed
1/2 tsp. sugar
3 T. soy sauce
1 tsp. garlic salt
1 1/2 T. wine
juice of fresh ginger root or 1/2
  tsp. ground ginger
1 tsp. salt

Marinate doves in mixture of all ingredients 2 hrs. Roll or shake in seasoned flour. Fry in deep fat until golden brown. Serve on rice.

JORDAN DOVE BREASTS (HAWAII)

12 dove breasts
1/2 c. pecan bits
2 c. orange juice
1/2 c. coconut bits
2 T. honey
4 slices crisp bacon, crumbled

Season breasts to your taste with salt and pepper. Marinate in orange juice and honey mixture 2 hrs. Fry bacon crisp, remove, brown meat in the drippings. Pour marinade over meat, cover, simmer 2 hrs. or until meat is tender. Add coconut and bacon as garnish. Thicken sauce, serve over hot buttered rice or noodles.

DOVE BREASTS IN SPAGHETTI SAUCE

6 or more dove breasts
1 jar spaghetti sauce
1/2 c. seasoned flour

Brown meat in margarine after shaking in seasoned flour. In large saucepan, place meat and cover with sauce, simmer 45 mins. Serve over spaghetti with 2 breasts per serving.

RAIL ROAST

Skin and clean birds, season with salt and pepper. Stuff with your favorite stuffing. Wrap bacon slices around bird. Roast at 400 degs. 30 mins. Baste frequently with butter.

FRIED RAIL

Split cleaned birds in half, season with salt and pepper. Dip in egg batter and fine bread crumbs, seasoned with a dash of marjoram. Sauté gently in butter about 15 mins. per side. Serve with lemon wedges, hot biscuits, tossed salad, and Indian pudding with whipped cream or ice cream.

BRAISED CROW

1 T. salt
1/2 c. sherry
2 T. vinegar
3 small onions, chopped
salt and pepper
1/4 c. celery, chopped
1/2 c. water

Clean and skin crows, soak meat in solution of salt and vinegar for 4-6 hrs. Split birds in half. Season with salt and pepper. Shake birds in flour, brown in half margarine, half bacon drippings. Pour off fat and add water, sherry, onions, and celery. Cover, simmer until tender.

ARIZONA B.B.Q. TURKEY

1/2 c. hot catsup
1/4 c. honey
2 T. cooking oil
2 T. vinegar
1/2 tsp. ground cloves
1/2 tsp. smoke flavored salt
1 10-12 lb. turkey, oven ready

Combine all ingredients but turkey. Blend well. Place turkey breast side up on rack or in shallow roasting pan. Brush well with sauce, basting frequently. Roast at 350 degs. about 3 hrs. or until tender. Should turkey become too brown, cover lightly with foil and continue roasting.

SANDHILL CRANE PIE

1 cleaned crane
3 whole cloves
1 bunch parsley, minced
1 c. cream
1 onion, chopped
buttermilk biscuits

Cut crane into serving pieces. Poach in water with parsley, onion, and cloves. When done, use either whole pieces or pick meat from bones. Strain water in which it was cooked. Make gravy adding cream or discard water and make a rich white cream sauce. Add meat to this gravy or sauce. Place in greased baking dish, top with buttermilk biscuits. Bake until biscuits are golden brown. Serve.

GROUSE DELITE

1 can mushroom soup
1 can mushroom stems and pieces
1 can cream chicken soup
1 med. onion, diced

Cut bird into serving pieces, dredge in seasoned flour, brown in skillet. Put in casserole. Mix with soups, mushrooms (include juice), and onion. Pour mixture over meat. Bake at 350 degs. for 1 1/2 hrs. Gravy from this is delicious served on rice or biscuits. Any upland game bird meat can be used.

ROASTED PRAIRIE CHICKEN

1 dressed prairie chicken
1/2 apple
handful celery leaves
melted butter or margarine

Wash chicken, pat dry. Stuff cavity with celery leaves and apple. Truss into shape. Roast at 425 degs. for 30-40 mins. Baste frequently with melted butter. Remove celery leaves before serving. Serves 2-3.

FRIED PRAIRIE CHICKEN

1 young prairie chicken
flour
salt and pepper
4 T. fat

Clean chicken, dress and cut into serving portions. Plunge into cold water, drain thoroughly, do not wipe dry. Season well with salt and pepper, dredge in flour, cook chicken slowly in hot fat. When chicken is brown and tender, about 1 hr., remove to a hot platter. Make cream gravy to serve with chicken.

ROAST BANDTAIL PIGEON

Clean, wash and stuff 2 to 4 birds as you would chickens, lay them in rows if roasted in the oven, with a little water in the pan to prevent them scorching. Unless they are real fat, baste with butter until half done, afterwards in their own drippings. Thicken the drippings, boil up once and pour in gravy boat. Place birds close together on dish, garnish with parsley.

BLACKBIRD BREASTS

bird breasts, cleaned and skinned
1 med. onion, chopped
2 carrots, sliced
1 can tomatoes
1 potato, diced
3/4 c. seasoned flour
1/2 c. celery, chopped

Sauté bird breasts in butter after dredging in seasoned flour. Combine all ingredients but breasts in Dutch oven and simmer in 1 c. water 30 mins. Add breasts and complete cooking. Thicken with seasoned flour. Serve over hot biscuits.

CASSEROLE OF PARTRIDGE

6 partridges
1/2 c. butter
6 thin slices ham
2 chicken bouillon cubes, dissolved
12 slices bacon
juice 6 oranges
1/2 c. brandy
salt and pepper

Line casserole with bacon slices. Stuff birds with favorite stuffing, truss. Cover breasts with bacon, and arrange in casserole. Place over low heat, covered. Allow to cook 15 mins. Pour brandy over birds. Cover and cook at 400 degs. for 20 mins. in oven. Remove birds and ham, keeping hot. Remove excess fat, discard. Strain remainder, add butter and stock to juices, stirring, bring to a boil. Season to taste. Add orange juice and blend. Return meat to sauce. Serve in casserole.

HAM-STUFFED PICKLED EGGS

6 beet-pickled hard boiled eggs cut
  in half lengthwise
1 tsp. prepared mustard
1/2 tsp. lemon juice
1/3 c. ground cooked ham
2 T. sweet pickle relish
1/2 tsp. Worcestershire sauce
2 T. salad dressing
dash salt and pepper

Remove yolks from eggs, mash yolks with a fork, blend in remaining ingredients, fill halves, chill thoroughly, serve with whole little beets or sliced beets.

CREAMED HAM AND EGGS

2 T. butter or margarine
1/2 tsp. salt
2 T. flour
dash pepper
2 c. milk
2 c. chopped or ground left-over ham
1 pkg. softened cream cheese
dash paprika
8 sliced hard cooked eggs

In a heavy fry pan, melt butter on medium heat, stir in flour, salt, pepper, gradually add milk, stirring until thickened; reduce heat to low, fold in cream cheese, eggs, and ham, just heat through; serve at once over biscuits, bannock, for breakfast. Makes 8 servings.

Notes

IV

Fish and Other Water Critters

SHARK STEAK

SHARK STEAK

4 shark steaks. Marinate steaks 1 hr. in white wine. Remove, dry, and grease with butter. Place on grill on greased foil square 4" above coals. Serve with baked potato, garlic toast, and tossed salad.

BOILED EELS

Use 4 small eels with sufficient water to cover, large bunch of parsley. Choose small eels for boiling. Put them in a stew pan with parsley, and just sufficient water to cover them. Simmer until tender, take them out, pour a little parsley and butter over them and serve in a tureen.

FRIED EELS

After cleaning eels well, cut them into 2" pieces, wash and wipe dry. Roll or shake in seasoned flour or cracker crumbs and fry as other fish in hot lard or drippings salted. They should be browned all over and thoroughly done. Eels may be prepared in this manner and broiled.

COLLARED EELS

Take 1 large eel, salt and pepper to taste, 2 blades of mace, 2 cloves, a little allspice firmly ground, 6 leaves of sage, small bunch of herbs minced very fine. Bone the eel, skin it, split it, and sprinkle over it with ingredients, taking care all spices are finely grounded, and herbs chopped very small. Roll it up and bind it with a broad piece of tape (linen). Boil it in water with salt and vinegar till tender. It may be served whole or cut in slices. When cold the eel should be kept in the liquid it was boiled in, but with a little more vinegar put to it.

EELS—LAMPREYS

Eels and lampreys should be fresh killed. To do so, jab the point of a fillet knife or ice pick in spine at base of head about 1" deep. Plunge lampreys into boiling water or scour with coarse salt to remove slime. With sharp knife, cut skin around head, loosen skin and draw down, tie cord about eel's neck looping over a nail or nail head directly to post. With pliers, grasp skin at neck, pull down and off in one motion. Cut head off, slit and clean, scrape off surface fat. Light tail fin bones may be pulled out by hand. Soft bone is easily removed, filleting is simple task. Slice down sides from backbone. Eels and lampreys may be fried, broiled, baked, or stewed according to recipe for fatty fish. Both good jellied, smoked, or pickled. Both parboiled in salt water prior to cooking.

DEEP FRIED LAMPREY

2 lbs. lamprey in 2" pieces
1 c. fine bread crumbs, seasoned
  with garlic
Court Bouillon
2 eggs
salt, pepper, or a dash of cayenne

Put lamprey into saucepan, add Court Bouillon to cover. Cover, bring to boil. Remove from heat, let stand 20 mins. Drain off liquid (do not lift fish up through it), pat dry with paper towel. Beat eggs until light. Dip each piece into egg and roll in bread crumbs, press firmly. Arrange in deep fry basket. Shake gently to get rid of loose crumbs. Deep fry or pan fry.

BROILED EEL

1-2 lbs. eel
lemon juice
salt and pepper
2 T. oil

Dress bone as for spitchcocked eel. Put on plate, season with salt and pepper, a sprinkle of lemon juice, and cooking oil on 3" lengths. Refrigerate until 20 mins. before serving time. Move eel to heated, greased broiling rack and broil until golden brown on both sides. Serve on warm platter, garnish. Serve sauces.

RICE-STUFFED CATFISH

6 skinned pan-ready catfish
1 T. oil
2 tsp. salt
1 T. orange juice
orange rice stuffing

Wash and pat fish dry. Sprinkle inside and out with salt and pepper. Fill with stuffing. Place in 9" x 13" x 2" pan. Mix remaining ingredients and brush fish with mixture. Bake in preheated 350 deg. oven for 25-30 mins. Serves 6.

BEER BATTER

1 12-oz. can light beer, 1 c. flour, 1 T. salt, 1 T. paprika. Beat with a whisk. Dip food in flour then in batter, fry in hot deep oil at 400 degs. until golden brown.

SALMON WITH SAUCE

2" long salmon steaks, 1/4 lb. butter, 1/5 tsp. chopped parsley, 1 shallot, salt and pepper and grated nutmeg to taste. Lay salmon in a baking dish; lay pieces of butter over it, and add other ingredients, rubbing a little of the seasoning into the fish, baste frequently. When done take it out and drain it for 1 or 2 mins. Lay it in a dish, pour sauce over it and serve. You may also use tomato sauce dressing.

BAKED SALMON

Clean fish, rinse it well, wipe dry, rub inside with lemon wedges, salt and pepper, now do the outside likewise. Fill with your favorite dressing, add sage and thyme to dressing if desired. Tie a thread around the fish to keep the dressing in. Lay a trivet in dripping pan, lay bits of butter over the fish, dredge with flour, place on trivet, 1 pt. hot water in drippings pan to baste with. A large fish bakes in 1 hr. in a quick oven, baste frequently. When the fish is taken up, having cut a lemon in very thin slices, put them in the pan, let them fry a little then dredge in a tsp. of wheat flour, add a small bit of butter, stir it about and let it brown without burning for a little while. Then add 1/2 c. or more of boiling water, stir it smooth, take the slices of lemon into the gravy boat and strain the gravy over. Serve with mashed potatoes, coleslaw, green beans with ham, cherry pie, coffee.

ATLANTIC SALMON

Atlantic salmon trout are treated as West Coast salmon.

BROILED SALMON

Cut some slices about 1" thick, and broil them over a hot, bright gentle fire of coals for 10-12 mins. When both sides are done take them on a hot dish, butter each slice well with sweet butter, strew over each a little salt and pepper to taste, serve hot.

BOILED SALMON

The middle slice of salmon is the best. Sew up neatly in mosquito netting bag and boil 1/4 hr. per lb. in hot salted water. When done unwrap with care and lay upon a hot dish, taking care not to break it. Have ready a large cupful of drawn butter, very rich, in which has been stirred a T. of minced parsley and the juice of a lemon, pour half over the salmon, serve the remainder in a gravy boat. Garnish with parsley and sliced eggs.

SHORE CABIN SALMON

Clean salmon good, stuff cavity with lemon wedges, tomato wedges, sliced green pepper, sliced fresh mushrooms, celery chunks, salt, and pepper. Preheat oven to 350 degs. Bake 1 hr. for fish up to 2 lbs. Serve on platter, garnish with parsley. If cooked on a grill, wrap in heavy duty foil. Lay directly on coals. Turn once, 30 mins. per side.

PICKLED COLD SALMON

Use liquid in which fish has been boiled, 3 breakfast cupsful, to which add vinegar to taste (a short teacupful), a good pinch of pepper, a dessert spoonful of salt. Boil a few mins. with a sprig of parsley and a little thyme. After it has become quite cold pour over the fish and allow to marinate for 1 hr. or so. Serve cold.

DRIED OR SMOKED SALMON (1886)

Cut the fish down the back, take out the entrails and roe, seal it, rub the outside with common salt; hang to drain 24 hrs. Pound 3 ozs. saltpeter, 2 ozs. course salt and 2 ozs. of course brown sugar. Mix well together, rub salmon over every part with it. Then lay on a large dish for 2 days. Then rub it over with common salt and in 24 hrs. it will be fit to dry. Wipe it well, stretch it open with stick skewers and hang it in a chimney with a smothered wood fire, or in a smoke house, or in a cool dry place. Shad may also be done in a like manner. They also make mighty fine eating.

CHESAPEAKE CRAB DIP

1 c. mayonnaise
1 tsp. lemon juice
1/2 c. sour cream
1 T. parsley, chopped
1 T. sherry
6 ozs. crab meat

Combine all ingredients, mix well. Chill thoroughly before serving. Makes 2 cups.

BOILED SHAD

Wash, wipe and split fish, sprinkle with salt
and pepper, lay on a buttered rack, inside
downward, when the lower side is brown, turn
the fish. A medium fish will be done in 20 mins.
Serve on hot plate with a good chunk of lemon
butter on it.

GATOR CHOWDER

alligator chunks
butter
2 onions, sliced thin
cream
2 white potatoes, sliced thin
salt and pepper
6 slices bacon
crumbled crackers

Lightly oil sides and bottom of adequate Dutch
oven. Place sliced bacon on bottom, gator
chunks on top, then onions and potatoes. Top
with crumbled crackers. Repeat layers until
ingredients are used up. Add water to half fill
oven. Cover, simmer slowly until done. Add
cream, cover again and cook 30 mins. longer.

FRIED GATOR TAIL

gator tail, boned
butter
seasoned flour

Slice gator tail across the grain. Dredge in
flour. Fry in butter until brown and tender.
Make a cream gravy if desired and immerse fried
pieces. Serve with hot rice, hot buttered
biscuits, and a salad.

SMOKED GATOR

alligator fillets
paprika
salt and pepper
prepared Italian dressing

Season gator fillets with salt and pepper and paprika. Marinate in the prepared Italian dressing for 2 hrs. Cover fire with smoked hardwood chips, smoke with low heat for about 3 hrs. or until completely done. Alligator is excellent when smoked in the traditional fashion.

TO FRY OR BOIL FISH PROPERLY

After the fish is well cleaned, lay it on a towel folded, and dry out all the water. When well wiped out and dry, roll it in wheat flour, rolled cracker crumbs, grated stale bread, or Indian meal, according to your preference. Wheat flour is generally liked. Have a heavy 10" skillet or spider, with plenty of sweet lard salted (1 T. salt to 1 lb. lard) for fresh fish that has not been previously salted. Let it become boiling hot, then lay the fish in it and let it fry gently until one side is a delicate brown, then turn the other. When both are done, take it up carefully and serve quickly, or keep it covered with a tin cover. Keep the dish where it's hot.

MOCK TURTLE EGGS

These are used in green turtle soup or in snapper soup. 6 T. catfish meat or turtle meat chopped fine, rub to a paste with the yolks of 2 hard boiled eggs. 1 T. butter, a little oyster liquor, season with cayenne mace. 1/2 tsp. white sugar, blend with a well beaten egg, slap into pellets the size and shape of turtle eggs, dip in beaten egg then cracker crumbs, fry in butter, drop into soup when it is served.

USING CRAYFISH

Allow 1 lb. per serving, sort out dead crayfish, discard. Crayfish will hold about 12 hrs. in a tub of clean water. Use a large kettle of boiling water with bay leaves, caraway seed, and salt. Drop live crayfish into boiling water, cook until crayfish turn bright red. Break off tails, peel, remove gall cysts and digestive tract. (When cool, can be done in 1 jerk.) Now either deep fry or use in cocktail.

FRIED CRAYFISH

1 qt. crayfish, boiled and cleaned
salt and pepper
1 egg
flour or cornmeal
1 1/2 c. milk
cooking oil

In bowl, combine egg, milk, salt, and pepper. Mix thoroughly. Dip crayfish into egg mixture, dust with flour or cornmeal, and drop into deep fat. Cook until golden brown. Serve as shrimp with lemon and your favorite sauce.

BROILED TROUT

Clean and split them open, season with a little salt and cayenne pepper. Dip in whipped egg, dredge in seasoned flour, broil over a clear, hot fire, serve with sauces.

TO FRY SMELT

Egg, bread crumbs, a little flour, boiling lard. Smelt should be very fresh, washed no more! Dry them on a cloth, lightly flour, dip in egg, sprinkle over with fine bread crumbs, place in boiling lard, fry to a nice pale brown. Be careful not to take off light roughness of crumbs, or their beauty is spoiled. Dry before the fire on a drainer. Serve with melted lemon butter.

OYSTERS STEWED WITH MILK

Take a pt. of fine oysters, put them with their own liquor and gill (1/4 pt.) of milk in a stew pan and, if you like, a blade of mace. Set it over the fire, take off any scum which may rise. When they are plump and white turn them into a deep plate, add a bit of butter and pepper to taste. Serve oyster crackers and dressed celery with them. Oysters may be stewed in their own liquor instead of milk.

PICKLED SHRIMP

- 1 lb. raw shelled shrimp
- 1 T. cayenne pepper
- 2 c. vinegar
- 1 T. celery seed
- 1 T. dry mustard
- 3 bay leaves

In the vinegar place all seasonings, bring to a boil, add raw shrimp. Boil 15 mins. or until shrimp can be speared with a fork. Place shrimp in sterilized jar, cover with liquid, seal, place in refrigerator. Improves with age. Will keep indefinitely.

FRIED OYSTERS

Take large oysters from their own liquor onto
a thickly folded napkin to dry them off, then
make a T. of lard or beef drippings hot in a
thick bottomed fry pan; add to it a salt
spoonful of salt. Dip each oyster in wheat
flour or fine bread crumbs till it will take
up no more. Then lay them in the pan, hold it
over a gentle fire until one side is done to
a delicate brown, turn the other by sliding a
fork under it. Takes 5 mins. to fry them after
they're in the pan. Best to fry them in lard.

FROG LEGS, FRIED

24 frog legs
1/4 c. shallots, chopped
seasoned flour
1/2 c. chopped parsley
oil
salt and pepper
2 T. butter
1/2 c. dry white wine
1 c. chopped mushrooms or 1 can
**   mushroom soup**

Skin out frog legs, roll in seasoned flour. Fry
in hot oil until golden brown. In pan, sauté
shallots in butter, add mushrooms or soup, and
parsley just until done. Season to taste. Place
meat on hot serving plate, cover with mushroom
mixture. Pour wine over all.

CHRISTMAS GAME PIE

This pie can be made with any of the game birds. Grouse and quail make a wonderful game pie. Clean, pluck and wash the birds; cut quail in half, grouse in 4 pieces. Trim off inferior pieces (necks, lower ribs, etc.). Put these with the giblets in a saucepan with 1 1/2 pts. of water. While this is stewing make a pastry crust. Line a large pudding dish or similar vessel, reserve enough dough for a lid at least 1" thick. When the livers are tender, take them out leaving the gravy to stew in the covered saucepan. Lard the breasts of the birds with tiny strips of salt pork; mince a couple slices with the livers, a bunch of parsley, sweet marjoram, and thyme also chopped fine. Juice a lemon, pepper and salt, a small shallot chopped. Make a farce-meat of this with bread crumbs, moistened with warm milk. Put some thin strips of corn beef or ham in the bottom of the pie next to the crust; lay upon these pieces of the birds peppered and buttered, then a layer of the farce-meat until you're ready for the gravy, strain this. Return it to the fire, and season with salt and pepper and a wine glass full of wine. Heat to a boil, pour into the pie, cover with the upper crust, cutting a slit in the middle. Ornament with pastry leaves arranged in a wreath about the edge. Place in the middle a pastry bird with bits of curled pastry about it. Bake these (separately). Lay on when pie is done. Bird will cover hole in the middle. Bake 3 hrs. for a large pie, covering with greased paper if it threatens to brown too fast.

CORN OYSTERS

oil
1/4 c. flour
2 c. fresh corn kernels (5 ears) or
  1 can cream style
1/2 tsp. salt
1/2 tsp. pepper
2 eggs, separated

Heat about 1/2" oil in 10-12" skillet. Combine corn, egg yolks, flour, salt, and pepper in medium bowl. In a separate bowl, beat egg whites until stiff peaks form, fold into corn mixture. Drop into oil by teaspoonsful, brown both sides. Turn once, drain on paper towels. Serve immediately.

PICKLED FISH

2 lbs. fish fillets
1/4 c. onion, chopped
1/2 c. vinegar
2 bay leaves
1/4 c. cooking oil
1 clove garlic, minced
1 4-oz. can green chiles
1 tsp. salt
1 T. orange peel, shredded
1/4 tsp. pepper
1/4 c. orange juice

Thaw fish if frozen. Place in 10" skillet, add boiling water to cover. Simmer 5-8 mins. or until fish flakes easily. Drain fish, arrange in shallow baking pan or dish. Combine vinegar, oil, chiles (rinsed, seeded, and chopped), orange peel, orange juice, onion, bay leaves, garlic, salt, and pepper. Pour over fish, cover. Refrigerate 3 hrs. Drain off marinade, cut fish into bite-size pieces. Garnish with orange slices. Serves 8-10.

CARP CARE

Carp is at its best when taken from cold water. It should be killed, bled out, skinned, and filleted immediately after catching. All tough dark meat is removed, cut in chunks, skin and bones removed, sprinkle with Kosher salt. Let stand 1 hr. but not less than 1/2 hr. before cooking.

PAN FRIED BLUE GILLS

Clean and scale fish, dredge in seasoned flour, season to taste. In a heavy skillet melt 1 stick margarine, brown fish lightly but not crisp, both sides over moderate heat until flesh flakes. Serve with melted butter over all.

CLAM CHOWDER

4 slices bacon, diced
3 potatoes, diced
2 onions, chopped fine
diced clams for 4 persons

Milk to cover; fry bacon crisp, add onion, potatoes, clams, salt and water to cover. Cook until potatoes are done. Heat milk separately. Ladle clam mixture into bowls, pour hot milk over it. Your clam mixture won't sour when it is left over.

PICKLING MARINADE FOR FISH

1 c. cider vinegar
1/4 c. water
2 T. brown sugar
1 lemon, thinly sliced
2 cloves garlic, sliced
1 bay leaf
1 pinch of nutmeg and sage
salt and pepper

Place in stainless steel pan. Cook 4 mins. over medium heat, bring to boil. Remove and cool. Pour over fish to be marinated. Refrigerate 2-3 days. Serve cold. Serves 4.

BASQUE STYLE HALIBUT

4 halibut steaks
seasoned flour
1 lemon
2 cloves garlic
salt and pepper
3 T. oil
1 egg

Squeeze the juice of the lemon over halibut steaks, sprinkle with salt and pepper. Dip into beaten egg, then seasoned flour. Shake off excess flour. Brown garlic cloves in oil. Remove garlic, add steak and cook over medium heat until lightly browned on both sides and fish flakes with a fork.

SMOKED CARP

In your smoker or smoke house, get your hickory, corn cobs, or apple wood ready. You will need both green and dry wood. When this is ready, go catch your carp. Mix enough salt in water to float an egg high enough to expose a tip about the size of a 5¢ piece. Submerge the carp cleaned and scaled in this brine. Place a hardwood disc over the fish to hold it down. Scrub a good-sized rock to place on top of disc. Let soak 24 hrs. Place fish on rocks in smoker and hot smoke for 12 hrs. Keep temperature 150-170 degs.. Brush cavity with cooking oil at start and once or twice during smoking. Wrap in foil and refrigerate several weeks.

FISH PRESERVING

This is used mostly on bony fish, but other fish can also be pickled. First scale, then cut off heads and tails of smaller fish. For the bigger ones, fillet. Cut into bite-size pieces. Soak in a brine solution or 2 c. pickling salt (uniodized), 1 gal. water for 48 hrs. Next, drain, rinse and pack in crock, glass container, or enamel ware, or small keg. Over this pour a mixture of half water, half vinegar, 1/2 tsp. each black pepper, white pepper, mustard seed, tarragon, bay leaf, pressed clove of garlic. Mix well then pour over layered fish and sliced onion. Allow to pickle in refrigerator 6-8 weeks or even 10 weeks.

SNAPPING TURTLE SOUP

Meat from 1 or more turtles in small chunks. Brown meat in bacon drippings, set aside. Make your favorite vegetable soup, add meat and simmer several hrs. or until meat is tender. Season with salt and pepper near end of cooking time.

ALASKAN RAZOR CLAM CHOWDER

1 c. raw clams, minced
4-6 potatoes, diced
4-6 carrots, diced
2 13-oz. cans milk
1 onion, diced
4 strips bacon
3 c. water

Fry bacon crisp in Dutch oven (4-qt. size).
Sauté onion, potatoes, and carrots in 3 T. of
the bacon grease. Add clams, cover with water,
cook until potatoes are tender. Cool, add milk
and the remaining water. Heat, do not boil.
Remove and serve. **NOTE:** After you have dug your
clams, leave them in salt water or beer for
several hrs. to clean themselves. A handful of
corn meal thrown in will also help the cleaning
process.

V

Liquid Concoctions

ARTILLERY
PUNCH

ARTILLERY PUNCH

1 fifth rye
1/2 pt. cognac
1 fifth claret
2 ozs. Benedictine
4 c. strong black tea
2 c. orange juice
1 pt. Jamaica rum
1 c. lemon juice
1/2 pt. gin or vodka
2 c. pineapple juice

Combine all ingredients. Let stand to ripen about 2 hrs. Pour over block of ice in punch bowl. Makes about 42 punch cups.

TESWIN

1 1/2 lbs. white corn
1 T. anise
5 panochas, crushed
6 sticks cinnamon
1 cake dry yeast
dry peel of 2 oranges
2 1/2 gals. water
15 cloves

Use crock, jug, or Mexican olla. Roast corn in oven or skillet on top of stove, stirring constantly until it turns a light brown. Set aside to cool, grind with coarse food chopper, wash in several waters. Discard hulls. Remove from water to crock. Add 3 sticks cinnamon; orange peels; add 2 pieces of sheeting, 1 for yeast and 1 for crushed anise, cloves, and 3 sticks cinnamon; tie tightly. Add panochas (brown sugar) and 4 butt ends of corn husks if available, add cold water. Put cloth cover over crock cover with lid. Leave 3 days and then stir with long-handled wooden spoon. Let sit again 2 days until the corn comes to the top. Strain and drink cold. POW! Apache crazy water.

PRICKLY PEAR WINE

```
6 lbs. fruit pulp
4 1/2 c. sugar
water
1 cake yeast
```

Burn spines from fruit, run fruit less the seeds through a coarse food chopper. For each 6 lbs. fruit pulp, add 2 c. water plus 1 for seeds and 1 for pulp. Bring to a boil, simmer 10 mins., set aside. Need 1 keg (size you want for wine), 2 gals. juice, sugar, and yeast. Place juice, sugar, and yeast in keg. Cork lightly with hose to a qt. jar of water on the floor. Put in cool 60-70 degs. After 3-6 weeks and bubbles have stopped coming out hose, let sit 1 week. Spoon off clear wine, wash keg, or jug. Return, let sit another week and siphon into sterilized bottles. Let age at least 6 weeks, longer is better.

ORANGE WINE

```
4 doz. oranges, peeled
5 gals. water
10 lbs. sugar
1 pt. brandy
```

Heat water and pour over orange peels. Let stand 3 hrs. Add strained juice of oranges. Now add sugar and brandy. Bottle and let stand 3 weeks to a month before sampling. WOW!

WILD GRAPE WINE

5 qts. shucked wild grapes, no stems. Crush and place in a crock with 1 qt. water per qt. grape pulp. Set aside to ferment. Add water to maintain level in the crock. When the contents stop working, strain through a muslin bag, return to crock and allow to work again. When it stops, siphon off and bottle.

ELDERBERRY WINE

1 qt. blossoms
2 oranges, sliced
2 lemons, sliced
1 qt. boiling water

Use fresh blossoms, no stems. Blossoms should be packed but not crushed. Add 2 sliced lemons, 2 sliced oranges, and 1 qt. boiling water. Let stand 24 hrs. Strain off liquid, add 1 c. sugar to each qt. of juice. Pour into uncovered jar. Once each day fill jars to top with reserved liquid. When fermentation ceases, strain wine and bottle tightly.

SPICED WINE

1 cinnamon stick
1 c. water
1 tsp. whole cloves
1 c. vodka
1 small piece (1/2" square) dried ginger root
3 c. dry red wine
1/2 c. blanched whole almonds
1/2 c. sugar and raisins

Tie spices in double layer of cheesecloth. Place in heavy saucepan with sugar and raisins. Cook 10 mins. over low heat, then cook about 30 mins. for real spicy flavor, remove spice bag. Add almonds, add vodka and wine at this point as needed.

STRAWBERRY WINE

3 qts. strawberries, mashed and strained. To the juice (about 1 qt.), if berries are fresh and ripe, add 1 qt. water, 1 lb. sugar, stir together well, allow to ferment in clean cask or crock, leaving the bung out. When it is through working, close tightly or rack off and bottle. A delicious drink.

DANDELION WINE

1 qt. blossoms
2 oranges, sliced
2 lemons, sliced
1 qt. boiling water

Use fresh blossoms, no stems. Blossoms should be packed but not crushed. Add 2 sliced lemons, 2 sliced oranges, and 1 qt. boiling water. Let stand 24 hrs. Drain off liquid. Add 1 c. sugar to each qt. juice. Pour into uncovered jars. Each morning fill to top with reserved juice. When fermentation ceases, strain wine and bottle tightly.

CURRANT WINE

Pick, stem and wash and strain currants, get very ripe ones.

1 qt. juice
1/2 pt. water
3/4 lb. white sugar

Stir all together long and well, put into clean cask, leaving out the bung. Cover the whole with a piece of mosquito netting. Let it ferment about 4 weeks. Back off and bottle when it is quite still.

RAISIN WINE

1 lb. white sugar
1 lemon, all the juice, half the
   peel
2 lbs. raisins, washed and chopped
2 gals. boiling water

Put all into a stone jar or crock. Stir every day for a week, then strain, bottle. It will be fit to drink in about 10 days.

CRANBERRY WINE

Mash ripe berries to a pulp, put in a stone jar or crock, add 1 qt. water to 2 qts. berries. Stir well, let stand 2 days. Strain through a double flannel bay. Mash a second supply of berries equal in quantity to the first and cover with this liquid, steep 2 more days and add 1 lb. sugar for 3 qts. of liquor. Boil 5 mins. Let it ferment in lightly covered jar, rack and bottle.

GINGER WINE

Take 1 qt. of 95% alcohol and put into it 1 oz. ginger root (bruised, not ground), 5 grains of capsicum, and 1 dram of tartaric acid. Let stand 1 week and filter. Now add 1 gal. of water in which 1 lb. of sugar has been boiled. Mix when cold. To make the color, boil 1/2 oz. cochineal, 3/4 oz. cream of tartar, 1/2 oz. alum in a pt. of water until you get a bright red color.

SLIPPERY ELM BARK TEA

Break the bark into bits, pour boiling water over it, cover, let it infuse until cold. Sweeten, ice and take for summer disorders, or add lemon juice and take for a bad cold.

BLACK BIRCH TEA

Steep a good handful of fresh new black birch twigs. Add sugar or honey as desired. Makes 1 qt. tea. Some people boil the twigs.

WILD MINT TEA

Take 1/2 c. crushed fresh mint plants, steep in 1 pt. water to taste. Add sugar if desired.

SHERPEE TEA

1 c. dry milk
1/4 c. sugar
1 tsp. instant tea

For each cup, 3 T. mix and a generous hunk of margarine in boiling water.

WATER CRESS TEA

1 T. water cress or roots, crushed
1 c. boiling water

Steep water cress and water. Add sugar to taste. Contains minerals.

KAHLÚA

3 c. water
3 c. sugar
10 tsp. instant coffee
4 tsp. vanilla
1 qt. cheap vodka

Simmer water, coffee, and sugar for 1 hr., let cool. Add vanilla and vodka. Yields 1 qt. 1 pt. coffee liquor.

WASSAIL

1 c. sugar
1 pt. fresh or frozen lemon juice
1/2 c. water
1 qt. red wine, "Rose" or burgundy
3 lemon slices
lemon slices for garnish
2 cinnamon sticks

Pour over ice in tall glass, add 2 c. cranberry juice.

HERB TEA FOR WHAT AILS YOU

Herb teas are made by infusing dried or green leaves and stems in boiling water and letting them stand until cold. Sweeten to taste.

SAGE TEA - sweetened with honey is good for a sore throat, and used as a gargle with a small bit of alum divided in it.

CATNIP TEA - is the best panacea for infant ills, in the way of cold and colic, known to nurses.

PENNY ROYAL TEA - will often avert the unpleasant consequences of a sudden check of perspiration or the evils induced by ladies' thin shoes.

CAMOMILE AND GENTIAN TEAS - are excellent tonics; taken with hot or cold blackberry root tea, said to be good for summer disorders.

TEA FROM GREEN STRAWBERRY LEAVES - is a soothing wash for a cankered mouth.

TANSY AND RUE TEAS - are useful in cases of colic.

FENNEL REED - steeped in brandy is also used for colic.

DAMASK ROSE LEAVES TEA - dry or fresh will usually subdue simple cause of summer complaint in children.

MINT TEA - made from the green leaves, crushed and settled in hot or cold water and sweetened, is palatable and healing to the stomach and bowels.

ARIZONA COWBOY EGGNOG

2 qts. prepared eggnog mix
1/2 qt. white rum
4 shots homemade apricot brandy
1 pt. vanilla ice cream

Makes 20 punch cups.

HOMEMADE BRANDY

2 lbs. apricots (1 pkg.)
1 qt. vodka
1 lb. wet rock candy

Use either 2 lbs. of home-cured apricots or 1 package store-bought fruit. Combine in a wide-mouthed gallon jar the fruit, wet rock candy, pour cheap vodka over all (1 pt. water). Set aside for 6 weeks. Fruit may be used several times. Bottle in convenient size for your use.

BLACKBERRY CORDIAL

4 qts. berries
2 tsp. cloves
1 qt. water
2 tsp. nutmeg
1 c. sugar
2 tsp. allspice
2 tsp. cinnamon
brandy or whiskey

Wash berries. Cook in water until mushy mixture results. Remove and strain. To this strained juice, add sugar. In a bag, put spices. Drop bag in juice and boil 15 mins. Remove from heat, cool. Add 1 pt. brandy or whiskey per qt. of juice. Pour into clean sterilized bottles, cap or cork. Good for diarrhea, mellows with age.

SALTY DOG

1 oz. gin or vodka
2 ozs. grapefruit juice

Rub rim of 6-oz. cocktail glass with peel of grapefruit, dip rim in Kosher salt. Fill glass almost full with shaved ice, or ice cubes. Add gin or vodka and freshly squeezed grapefruit juice. Stir well, serve.

COLONIAL HOT BUTTERED CIDER

8 c. cider
8 cinnamon sticks, 16 whole cloves
1 orange, thinly sliced
1 1/2 c. dark rum
1/2 c. honey
8 pats sweet butter

Using a saucepan heat cider, orange, honey, whole spices until bubbly. Simmer about 10 mins. Pour cider into heat proof mugs, add a cinnamon stick to each mug. Add rum to mugs, top with a pat of butter. Stir until butter melts. Serve hot.

HOT MULLED CIDER

1 qt. cider
1 tsp. whole cloves
1/4 c. brown sugar
1 tsp. allspice
2 sticks cinnamon

Use either hot spiced cider mix (available at supermarket) or simmer cider with your own mix, bagged at home. Float orange slices in bowl.

MOLASSES CANDY

1 c. molasses
pinch of salt
1 c. water

Combine molasses, water, and pinch of salt. Boil ingredients (do not stir) to hard boil stage. Remove from fire, but let stand until cool enough to handle in well greased hands. After pulling for some time, it turns from brown to a yellowish color. Cut into pieces.

HUNTER'S TODDY

3 c. beef bouillon
1/4 tsp. cinnamon
2 c. apple juice
1/4 tsp. cloves
1 c. water
1/4 tsp. nutmeg
1/2 c. brandy

In saucepan, combine all ingredients, bring to a boil, reduce heat, simmer 2 mins. to blend. Serve in mugs with orange slices. Makes about 9 cups.

SPECIAL OCCASION PUNCH

1 large can pink frozen lemonade
1 bottle champagne
1 small can frozen orange juice
1 qt. vodka
1 large bottle ginger ale
1/2 c. sugar
1 box fresh or frozen strawberries

Clean strawberries if fresh. Pour punch over ice then add champagne.

INDIAN WHISKEY (LONG AGO)

40 gals. proof spirits, 2 twists of tobacco, 1 bar yellow soap, shaved, 20 red peppers. After 4 days of sitting and stirring occasionally, strain and divide in 2 casks. Add water to fill the casks. Let set 24 hrs. and it is ready for sale. 1 tin cup half full equals 2 prime beavers.

CHERRY BOUNCE

4 lbs. sweet cherries and the same amount of sour cherries
2 1/2 lbs. white sugar
1 gal. whisky

Crush the cherries to pieces by pounding in a deep wooden vessel with a smooth billet of wood. Beat hard enough to crack all the cherry stones. Put into a deep stone jar. Mix in the sugar well, cover with the whisky. Shake around briskly and turn into a demijohn. Cork tightly and let stand a month, shaking it every day, then another month without touching it. Now strain off and bottle. It is better a year than 6 months old.

MONONGAHELA WHISKEY

To 40 gals. proof spirits, add 2 ozs. spirit of niter, 4 lbs. dried peaches, 4 lbs. N.O. sugar, 1 qt. rye (burned and ground like coffee), 1/4 lb., allspice, 1/2 lb. cinnamon, 1/2 lb. cloves. Put in all ingredients; after standing 5 days, draw it off and strain the same if necessary.

RASPBERRY ROYAL

4 qts. ripe berries
1 lb. white sugar
1 qt. cider vinegar
1 pt. fine brandy

Put the berries in a stone jar, pour the vinegar over them. Add the sugar and pound the berries to a paste with a wooden pestle, or mash with a spoon. Let them stand in the sun 4 hrs., strain and squeeze out all the juice and put in the brandy. Seal up in bottles. Lay them on their sides in the cellar, and cover with sawdust. Stir 2 T. of supply into a tumbler of ice water when you wish to use it.

HAYMAKERS SWITCHEL

A thirst quencher for the haying season:

    8 c. water
    1/2 c. molasses
    1 c. sugar
    1/2 tsp. ground ginger
    1/2 c. cider vinegar

In a saucepan heat together, water, sugar, vinegar, molasses and ginger until sugar is dissolved. Chill before serving. If being sent to the field, chill stone jug in the spring house, makes about 18 4-oz. cups. The jug was sometimes kept cool hanging in the well. It has been known to be spiked with brandy or whiskey.

HAIL STORM JULEP

Several sprigs of mint, slightly bruised in a tumbler with a teaspoon, put in a generous tsp. of sugar, add gradually stirring and rubbing lightly with enough water to fill the glass 3/4 full. Fill up with pounded ice, stir hard. Pour into large glass that you may shake up well and put in 2 T. or more of fine brandy.

VI

Vegetable Treats

COWBOY
BEANS

COWBOY BEANS

1 lb. pinto beans
1 6-oz. can tomato paste
2 1/2 c. cold water
1 tsp. chili powder
1/2 lb. salt pork, cubed
1 tsp. salt
1 red chili pepper
1 tsp. cumin seed
1 med. onion, chopped
1/2 tsp. marjoram
1 clove garlic, minced

Pick and wash beans, place in bowl, cover with cold water. Soak overnight. Next day place in Dutch oven, bring to boil, reduce heat, cover. Simmer 1 hr. Add remaining ingredients. Cover and simmer 3 hrs. or until done. Add water as necessary.

PAINTED DESERT BEANS

1/2 lb. sliced bacon
1/2 tsp. prepared mustard
1 lb. ground venison
1 tsp. salt
1/2 c. onion, diced
1 can lima beans, drained
1/2 c. brown sugar
1 can kidney beans, drained
1/2 c. hot B.B.Q. sauce
1 can pork and beans

Fry bacon until crisp, brown onion in drippings, pour off excess grease. Brown venison. Combine all ingredients in Dutch oven. Mix well, bake at 300 degs. covered 1 1/2 hrs.

TANGY BEANS

1 lb. pinto beans
1 large onion
salt and pepper
1 green pepper
1 c. prepared B.B.Q. sauce
1 c. brown sugar
1 lb. sliced bacon

Wash and cook beans until done. Dice pepper and onion. Fry bacon crisp, crumble. When beans are done, add remaining ingredients and cook 15 mins. longer. Serve with any game meat. 1 T. prepared mustard may be added if desired

MESQUITE BEANS

The mesquite bean is high in protein, also fat. When boiling the beans, you can skim off the fat to be used later as an oil. Also contains some calcium and about 70 calories per serving.

THREE-BEAN CASSEROLE

1/2 c. onion, chopped
1/2 c. catsup
1 T. oil
2 T. brown sugar, packed
1 16-oz. can kidney beans, drained
2 T. molasses
1 16-oz. can lima beans, drained
1/2 tsp. salt
1 20-oz. can baked beans

In a large saucepan, sauté onion in oil until lightly browned. Stir in remaining ingredients. Bring to boil over medium heat, stirring occasionally. Simmer 10 mins. to blend flavors. Serves 4. Crusty bread, coleslaw, potato bread, sausage or hot dogs grilled, cold milk, coffee, and watermelon make for an Old Fashioned July 4th picnic.

CRANBERRY BAKED BEANS

2 c. navy beans
1 T. Worcestershire sauce
8 c. cranberry juice cocktail
1 tsp. chili powder
1 can cranberry jelly, strained
1 tsp. dry mustard
1 c. onion, chopped
1/2 tsp. pepper
1 T. vinegar
4 ozs. salt pork chunk
1 T. lemon juice

In saucepan, combine beans and 6 c. cranberry juice cocktail. Simmer uncovered about 1 1/2-2 hrs. or until beans are tender. Add water from time to time as needed to prevent sticking. Drain beans, pour into 2 qt. casserole. Stir in remaining cranberry juice, cranberry jelly, onion, vinegar, lemon juice, Worcestershire sauce, chili powder, mustard, and pepper. Place salt pork on top. Cover and bake in preheated 300 deg. oven for 2 hrs. Remove lid and continue baking 1 hr. or until liquid is almost all absorbed. Serve with hot bread, coleslaw, and potato salad. Serves 8.

BEAN HOLE BEANS

Dig your pit twice the size of your 10" Dutch oven, put in a hard wood or charcoal fire, maintain for at least 8 hrs., rake out all unburned charcoal, or line pit with dry rocks for 2 hrs. of firing, rake out embers, place oven in pit. Lid on, cover with coals then dirt. To prepare and cook beans, pick and clean beans, take 2 1/2 c. presoaked navy beans, parboil until skin splits, cover with water, add 1 T. salt, 1/2 lb. diced bacon, 1/3 c. molasses, 1 tsp. dry mustard. Bring beans to a boil, cover and place pot in preheated pit for at least 8 hrs. Build a fire atop pit, allow to burn out.

LIMA BEAN BAKE

2 c. dried limas
1/4 c. cooking oil
1/2 lb. smoked ham, cubed
2 c. stewed tomatoes
2 tsp. salt
3/4 tsp. chili powder
1/2 c. onion, chopped
shredded cheddar cheese
1/4 c. green pepper, chopped

Wash beans, add 1 1/2 qts. water, bring to boil. Simmer 1 1/2 hrs. or until tender. After 1 hr., add salt. Sauté onions and pepper in oil until tender. Add tomatoes, chili pow-der, beans, and ham. Season with salt and pep-per to taste. Pour into casserole, sprinkle with cheese. Bake at 350 degs. 25 mins. Serves 8.

CRAZY BEANS

1 med. apple, sliced
1/4 c. raisins
1/2 c. chopped onion
2 T. catsup
1 32-oz. can pork and beans
2 T. prepared mustard
6 ozs. smoked sausage links
dash of cayenne
4 slices bacon, crisp and crumbled

Bake in 1 1/2 qt. bean pot in 375 deg. oven 1 hr. 15 mins. Serve hot with salad, game steak.

GOLD CREEK CALICO BEANS

1 lb. ground big game meat
1/2 c. brown sugar
1/2 lb. sausage
1/2 c. catsup
1 large onion, chopped
2 tsp. salt
1 32-oz. can kidney beans
2 T. vinegar
1 32-oz. can lima beans
1 tsp. dry mustard
1 32-oz. can baked beans

Brown meats together in large pan. Add onion, continue to cook until onion is soft. Add remaining ingredients, stir, mix well, cover. Bake in 350 deg. oven 40-60 mins. Serves 8.

LEATHER BRITCHES BEANS

Sometime during the winter, take a string of dried green beans down. Remove the thread and drop them into a pot of scalding water. Add a hunk of game meat. Cook all morning.

MARSH MARIGOLDS (SURVIVAL FARE)

This is an early edible green. But do not eat raw as it contains Kelleborin, a poison. This is destroyed by cooking. Collect leaves, smooth stems, before flowers appear. The long white roots are gathered and boiled for eating.

WILD ONION SOUP

Using 2 c. game broth, 2 c. diced potatoes, 1/2 c. chopped wild onions, combine all. Simmer until potatoes are done. Add a mixture of 2 T. flour, 2 tsp. drippings or butter, 1 c. broth, stir in until desired thickness is reached. Serves 4. Serve with hot biscuits.

DANDELION GREENS
(From Aunt May, bless her heart.)

In the pasture pick young dandelion greens.
After they have flowered they are too tough.
Wash the leaves real well, discard dark outside
leaves. Fry up some diced salt pork, or good
smoked bacon butt, add a small dried onion, now
add to the meat a mixture of 1/2 c. water,
1/2 c. vinegar, salt, pepper to taste, for each
qt. of greens. Pour solution over greens to
wilt them, serve at once.

INDIAN SUCCOTASH

This is made from green corn and lima beans,
although you can substitute other white beans.
Have a third more corn than beans. When the corn
is cut from the cob, and beans shelled, put into
boiling water enough to cover them. Stew gently
together until tender about 1/2 hr. Stir now
and then. Pour off nearly all the water, add
a large cupful of milk. Stew in this, watching and stirring to prevent burning, for 1 hr.
Then stir in a great lump of butter, a teacup
of flour wet with cold water or milk, pepper,
salt to taste. Boil up once and pour it into
a deep vegetable dish. Serve hot.

FRIED GREEN TOMATOES

4 med. fresh green tomatoes
1/2 c. seasoned bread crumbs or
   cracker crumbs
salt
2 beaten eggs
1/2 c. margarine

Remove core from tomatoes, cut in 1/2" slices,
sprinkle with salt. Dip slices in eggs and
crumbs, fry in margarine in large skillet until
browned. I prefer the tomatoes with a slight
blush. Serves 4-6.

GRILLED CORN

Dip unhusked corn in ice water. Place 4-5"
above coals or at edge of cooking fire. Grill
until husks blacken, 10-20 mins. Turn frequently to cook evenly. Using gloves, remove
husks with quick pulling motion. Serve immediately with butter, salt, and pepper.

BAKED MUSHROOMS

Place some large flat ones nicely cleaned and
trimmed on thin slices of well buttered toast,
putting a little nugget of butter in each one,
or also a snuff of pepper and salt. Lay them
on a baking tray, cover them carefully. Heap
the hot ashes upon them and let them bake on
the hearth for 15-20 mins.

PICKLED SUNCHOKES
(JERUSALEM ARTICHOKES)

2 1/2 c. chokes, chopped
1 1/2 c. green pepper, chopped
1/2 c. pimento, chopped
1/2 c. onion, chopped
1 c. white wine vinegar
2 1/4 tsp. salt
3 T. honey

Blend all in saucepan. Bring to boil, simmer
5 mins. Add vinegar, honey to taste. Nets 2 pts.

SUCCOTASH (BACON-BEEF)

6 slices bacon
1 17-oz. can whole kernel corn
1 med. onion, chopped
1 16-oz. can lima beans, drained
1 lb. lean ground venison
1 tsp. salt
2 bouillon cubes
1/2 tsp. pepper
1 c. water
dash sugar

In large skillet, cook bacon crisp, drain on paper towels, then crumble. Pour off all but 2 T. drippings. Add onion and venison and sauté, stirring until onion is tender and meat is brown. Add broth of bouillon cubes and water, corn and lima beans. Season with salt, pepper, and sugar. Cover and heat through. Serve in bowls, sprinkle with crumbled bacon.

MOCK CORN ON THE COB

Gather cattail flower stalks before pollen sits on. Husk off sheaths. Place in salted boiling water a few mins. until tender. Use plenty of margarine, salt, and pepper, if desired. Just like real corn!

PANHOS

1 c. cornmeal
1 lb. big game meat, ground or
   homemade sausage
1 med. onion, chopped fine
1 c. boiling water
1/2 c. ground nut meats

Mix water and cornmeal. Add all other ingredients. Place in bread pan. Chill, slice, and fry. Serve with butter, syrup, jam, and eggs.

SHOOFLY PIE

1 1/2 c. flour, sifted
1/4 c. margarine
1/2 c. sugar
1/2 tsp. baking soda
1/8 tsp. salt
1/2 c. unsulphured molasses
1/2 tsp. cinnamon
3/4 c. boiling water
1/4 tsp. ginger
1 unbaked 8" pastry shell
1/4 tsp. nutmeg

Mix together flour, sugar, salt, cinnamon, ginger, and nutmeg. In a bowl, cut in butter until mixture resembles course meal. Mix together baking soda and molasses and immediately stir in boiling water, stir in 1 1/3 c. crumb mixture. Pour into pastry shell. Sprinkle remaining crumb mixture over top. Bake at 375 degs. 30-40 mins. until crust is lightly browned. Serves 6-8.

POKE GREENS
(Good Old Aunt May Again!)

When the young stalks are no longer than a man's little finger, and show only a tuft of leaves at the top only a few inches above the ground, is the time to gather them. They aren't fit for table when larger. Scrape the stalk but do not cut off the leaves. Lay in cold water with a little salt for 2 hrs. Tie in bundles as you do asparagus, put into a saucepan of boiling water and cook fast 3/4 hr., lay buttered toast in a dish; untie the bundle, pile the poke evenly upon it, buttering very well, sprinkle with salt and pepper. This is a tolerable substitute for asparagus.

SWEET POTATO POI

Boil sweet potatoes in jackets until tender.
Peel, mash, beat until smooth, season to taste
with salt and pepper. Gradually beat in enough
coconut milk to get desired thickness. 1-2-3
finger poi. Keep hot. Serve in bowls.

CATTAIL ASPARAGUS

Cut off bottom 8-12" of cattail root stalk.
Peel off outside sheath to white or light green
centers. Cook in salted water until tender.
Serve hot as asparagus.

Notes

VII

Nuts, Seeds, Blossoms

ROASTED
SUNFLOWER
SEEDS

ROASTED SUNFLOWER SEEDS

Use a fully ripe flower head, shake out seeds. Roast in a dry skillet or baking sheet in oven. Sprinkle seeds with salt before roasting. Bake in slow oven 275-300 degs. 30-60 mins., stirring frequently for even toasting. Cool, crack, store as piñon nuts. Sunflower seed is about 1/2 protein and 1/2 oil, contains good amount of Vitamin B-6. **SUGGESTION**: Roast a large ripe head of seeds. Remove kernels. Use in cakes, gravies, stuffings, salads, etc.

HICKORY NUTS

Remove from shell. Use in candies, cakes, cookies, etc. Very rich flavor.

SPICED CASHEWS, BUTTERNUTS

2 T. melted butter
1 tsp. cinnamon
2 c. nut meats
1 tsp. allspice
3/4 c. granulated sugar
1/2 tsp. ginger

Put butter and nut meats in heavy iron skillet. Fry slowly for 20 mins., stirring occasionally. Mix granulated sugar, cinnamon, allspice, and ginger. Remove nuts and, while still hot, sprinkle with spice mixture.

ROASTED PUMPKIN SEEDS

Roasted and shelled, they add to candies, cakes, soups, and gravies.

CAROB NUT CANDY

Make your favorite fudge, put in carob powder and nuts.

WALNUTS

Remove from shell. Use in candies, cakes, cookies, salads, gravies, and breads.

SPICED WALNUTS

2 T. butter
1 tsp. cinnamon
2 c. walnut halves
1 tsp. ground allspice
3/4 c. sugar

At home, melt butter in shallow pan. Add walnut halves. Roast 25 mins. at 300 degs. Stir occasionally. Mix sugar, cinnamon, and ground allspice. Remove nuts from oven and sprinkle with spice mixture while still warm.

PEANUTS

Roast in butter and salt. Use in dressing, salads, gravies, soups, candy, etc.

ROASTED SPICED PEANUTS

1 1/2 tsp. salt
1 lb. raw blanched peanuts
3/4 tsp. Chinese 5 spice powder

Dissolve salt in 1/4 c. hot water, mix with spice powder. Pour peanuts and spice mixture together in suitable roasting pan; mix well, spread nuts out flat, roast in 275 deg. oven 1 hr. or until nuts are light brown. Stir nuts frequently for even roasting. When thoroughly cool, store in glass jars for future use.

FRIED PUMPKIN OR SQUASH BLOSSOMS

1 egg
milk
1/2 c. flour

Make a thin batter using egg, flour, and milk.
Dip blossoms in it and deep fry in hot grease.
Serve as other vegetables.

HERB BLEND

1 T. basil, dried, crushed fine
1 bay leaf, crushed fine
1 T. English thyme, dried
2 T. marjoram
1 T. parsley, dried
1 T. celery leaves, dried
1 1/2 tsp. rubbed sage

Blend together and store in dry containers. Use
for meats, poultry, soups, and gravies.

INDIAN ACORN STEW

2 lbs. lean game chunks
1 tsp. salt
1 c. ground acorn meal

Add water to cover meat chunks, cook until
tender. Be sure of water level during cooking.
Cook until tender and add salt. When meat is
done, separate from stock. Chop chunks fine to
tenderize. Add acorn meal to meat, mix well.
Pour stock over all, stir; serve hot over
noodles, hot biscuits, or rice.

POP CAKES

Grind buttered popcorn, salted, into meal in
hand grinder. Add milk or water and fry like
hot cakes.

CHESTNUTS

Slash flat side of nut. Place cut side up on baking sheet. Roast at 400 degs. about 20 mins. or until tender. Use fork in slash to test for tenderness.

PIÑON NUTS

From piñon pine. Use in cakes, cookies, soups, and gravies.

PEANUT BUTTER POPCORN

3 qts. popcorn
1/2 c. light corn syrup
1 1/2 c. nut meats
1 c. peanut butter
1 c. sugar
1 tsp. vanilla
1/2 c. honey

In a large roasting pan, combine popcorn and nut meats. Keep warm in 250 deg. oven. Butter sides of heavy 1 1/2 qt. saucepan. Combine sugar, honey, and corn syrup in pan. Bring to boil, stirring constantly. Boil hard 2 mins. Remove from heat, stir in peanut butter and vanilla. Quickly pour over popcorn mixture. Stir to cool well. Cool, break into bite-size pieces. Makes 3 qts. **SUGGESTION:** Use dry roasted peanuts, cashews, or mixed nuts in place of almonds, shelled sunflower seeds, pumpkin seeds, piñon nuts, separately or mixed.

PECANS

Crack shell, remove nut meat. Many baking uses also in candy, ice cream, and salads.

SWEET ACORNS

Ground as additive to flour in bread. Makes heavy cake.

VIII

Fruits & Berries.

PRICKLY
PEAR JELLY

PRICKLY PEAR JELLY (ALSO SAGUARO)

2 1/2 c. juice
1 pkg. pectin
4 c. sugar
1/3 c. lemon juice
1 tsp. strawberry or raspberry
  flavoring

Need fruit to make 2 1/2 c. juice. Singe fruit over flame, wash, quarter, put in pan. Cover with water, boil 15-20 mins. Let cool slightly. Strain off juice. Add sugar, strawberry or raspberry flavoring, pectin, and lemon juice. Boil hard 1 min. Add flavoring and put in sterilized sealed jars.

OAHU PINEAPPLE

1 can pineapple chunks (2 1/2 size)
salted roasted cashews
2/3 c. sour cream
shredded coconut
1 T. brown sugar

In serving bowl, place pineapple chunks. In another bowl, mix sour cream and brown sugar. Spoon over pineapple chunks. Just before serving, sprinkle with salted roasted cashews and shredded coconut. Serves 4.

CRANBERRY APPLESAUCE LEATHER

1 16-oz. can cranberry sauce
1 30-oz. can applesauce

Mix the 2 fruits together real well. Then dry as basic leather, but use 2 pans. The 2 thin leathers will be quite moist and sticky because of the high sugar content of sauces.

ELDERBERRIES

Many foragers prefer the flowers to the berries. The flowers are in clusters of flat white flowers. They are used for tea, wine, syrup, vinegar, flavoring, and fritters. Also as ingredients in fritters, muffins, pancakes, custards, tarts, hand creams and face creams. The berries mixed with scarlet sumac along with reddish-brown seed clusters must be soaked in cold water to remove hair on the berries. Mixed half and half, elderberry and scarlet sumac will make real jelly.

TREELESS MAPLE SYRUP

6 med. potatoes
1 c. brown sugar
1 c. white sugar
2 c. water

Peel and boil potatoes in 2 c. water until half the liquid has boiled away. Remove potatoes, use as you want. Heat liquid until it boils again. Slowly add sugars. Boil until all sugar is dissolved. Remove from heat, allow to cool, set aside in cool dark place a few days for best flavor.

SHERRIED PRUNES

Soak prunes in sherry. Stuff each with 1/2 walnut, wrap in 1/2 slice bacon. Broil on skewers on grill until bacon is crisp.

DRIED FIGS

Dip figs in boiling water for 1 min., spread fruit 1 layer only on screen wire or slotted trays. Cover with cheesecloth or any open fabric. Place in well circulated area, not in hot sun. Dry until leathery stage; skin will become glossy and slightly sticky. To shorten drying time and to keep insects away, use an electric fan. Store in glass jars or food bags, where it is cool.

MULBERRY PIE

The fruit of the mulberry resembles the blackberry in color and shape. When ripe it is a dark purple. It will make a wonderfully rich pie. Fill an unbaked pie shell, fill it with fruit, sprinkle it with sugar, mix with 1/4 c. flour, juice of lemon, add top crust, bake in 375 deg. oven 50 mins. or until crust is brown. Serve with cold milk or lemonade.

GOOSEBERRY FOOL

1 qt. ripe gooseberries
yolks of 4 eggs
1 T. butter
meringue of whites and 3 T. sugar
1 c. sugar

Stew the gooseberries in just enough water to cover them. When soft and broken, rub them through a sieve to remove the skins; while still hot beat in the butter, sugar and whipped yolks of eggs. Pile in a glass dish, or in small glasses, heap upon the top a meringue of the whipped whites and sugar.

BAKED PAPAYA

1/4 c. sugar
1 tsp. curry powder
1 1/2 tsp. cinnamon
1/2 c. water chestnuts, thinly
   sliced
1 1/2 c. cottage cheese
2 T. white seedless raisins
1 8-oz. or 2 3-oz. pkgs. softened
   cream cheese
3 papayas, halved and seeded
1/4 c. butter, melted
2 T. chutney, chopped

Preheat oven to 450 degs. Mix cinnamon and sugar thoroughly, set aside. Combine cottage cheese, cream cheese, chutney, and curry powder until well mixed. Stir in water chestnuts and raisins. Spoon into the papaya halves. Place papayas in baking dish. Pour melted butter over each and sprinkle with cinnamon and sugar. Bake 15 mins. Serves 6.

BASIC FRUIT LEATHER

1 30-oz. can of applesauce. Coat a 11" x 16" cookie sheet with non-grease spray or stick spread. Spread applesauce evenly on the sheet so that it is no more than 1/4" thick. Dry the fruit puree in a slow oven, about 150 degs., with the door open a crack for 6-8 hrs. When dry the leather will be translucent, pliable and body sticky. Peel the fruit leather from the pan, roll and slice it into 8 small rolls. Each roll will be the equivalent of 1/2 c. of fruit. Makes a fine trail snack. Nuts and spices may be added to boost up the flavor. Stores well in large air-tight jars.

PRICKLY PEAR OR SAGUARO FRUIT PIE
(This is a real way out West dish.)

4 c. prickly pear pulp
dough for 2 9" pie shells
1 1/4 c. sugar
1 tsp. corn starch
1 tsp. cherry flavoring

Mix pulp, sugar and corn starch in large mixing bowl with flavoring. Pour mixture into pie shell, cover top with strips of dough in lattice formation. Bake at 350 degs. about 1 hr. or until done.

ELDERBERRY—SUMAC JELLY

2 c. elderberries
1 box pectin
2 c. sumac
5 c. sugar

Soak and squeeze sumac. Bring first 3 ingredients to a boil. Add sugar, boil 1 min. or until it tests right for jelly that will be clear red.

PYRACANTHA JELLY

1 pt. pyracantha berries
1/4 c. lemon juice
3 qts. water
1 pkg. powdered pectin
5 1/2 c. sugar
3/4 c. fresh grapefruit juice

Boil berries and water 20 mins., add lemon and grapefruit juice. Bring to a rolling boil, add sugar all at once, boil 2 mins. more. Skim if necessary, pour into hot sterile jars and seal.

BLACKBERRY OR RASPBERRY SLUMP

Slump is a sort of deep dish pie or cobbler made on top of the stove. Pick over and wash your berries. Usually used with sugar and cream or ice cream.

      1 1/4 c. sugar
      1/4 tsp. salt
      1/4 c. shortening
      1 c. boiling water
      1/2 c. milk
      1/4 tsp. cinnamon
      1 1/2 c. sifted flour
      1 T. cornstarch
      1 1/2 tsp. baking powder
      3 c. fresh berries

Cream 1/2 c. sugar and shortening, add milk, blend well, stir in flour, salt and baking powder together; combine with shortening mixture, set aside. In a saucepan combine remaining sugar, cinnamon and corn starch. When blended gradually add water, simmer stirring constantly. When thickened gently add berries, folding into the syrup. Drop dabs of butter on top of berry mixture, cover, cook at same heat for 10 mins. or until batter is steamed through. Serve with cream or vanilla ice cream.

ROLY POLY

Take 1 qt. flour, make a good biscuit crust; roll out to 1/2" thick, spread with any kind of fruit or preserves, fold so fruit will not run out, dip a cloth into boiling water, flour it and lay around the pudding closely, leave room to swell, steam 1 1/2 hrs. Serve with boiled sauce.

FIREPLACE BANANAS

banana
1 T. semi-sweet chocolate
orange juice
6-8 miniature marshmallows
cinnamon

Peel back a 1" strip from banana. Make a slit
lengthwise, brush with orange juice, sprinkle
lightly with ground cinnamon. Fill slit with
semi-sweet chocolate, and 6-8 miniature marshmallows. Roll peel back over banana. Wrap in
foil, place on or near burning embers 5-10
mins. until marshmallows are melted. Roll back
foil and enjoy.

IX
Breads, Butters, Sauces, Puddings

DESERT RATS
SOUR DOUGH
STARTER

DESERT RATS SOUR DOUGH STARTER

2 c. flour
2 c. lukewarm water
3 T. sugar
1 tsp. salt
1 pkg. dry yeast

In clean, scalded crock or keg, place ingredients. Stir until mixture is a smooth thin paste. Put on lid and set in warm place to sour. Stir several times a day. Should be ready in 2-3 days. If you do not have yeast, use 4 T. sugar and 1 1/2 tsp. salt, but let set 5 days.

IRISH SODA BREAD

4 c. flour
1/4 c. sugar
1 tsp. salt
1 tsp. baking powder
1/4 c. margarine
1 1/2 c. currants
2 med. eggs, slightly beaten
1 1/3 c. buttermilk
1 tsp. baking soda

Sift first 4 ingredients together into a mixing bowl, cut in margarine with pastry blender until mixture looks like corn meal; stir in currants, mix together remaining ingredients, stir into flour until well moistened. Do not over mix. Turn butter into greased 2 qt. round casserole or souffle dish, cover with towel, bake at 375 degs. for 50 mins. Allow to stand 10 mins. Remove to cooling rack. Makes 1 loaf.

HUNTER FRIED BREAD

Make your bread from Bisquick Mix. Fry over low heat with just enough bacon drippings to cover the bottom of your skillet. Roll in sugar for doughnuts.

SCOTCH SHORT BREAD

2 c. sifted flour
1 c. margarine
1 c. cornstarch
1/2 c. sugar
pinch of salt

Stir together flour, cornstarch, salt, in a mixing bowl. Blend margarine and sugar until light and fluffy. Add dry ingredients gradually until dough is stiff enough to work with the hands. Knead on slightly floured board until well blended and smooth. Press into 12"x8" rectangular pan, smooth over top, score almost through with knife into 1"x2" blocks, prick with a fork. Bake in 325 deg. oven 30-40 mins. or until golden brown. Recut rectangles and sprinkle with sugar while still hot. Cool completely, remove from baking sheet. Store in air tight container. Makes 4 doz. 1"x 2" rectangles.

BASQUE SHEEPHERDER BREAD

This loaf is a large dome-shaped loaf of bread. It is the herder's staff of life along with beans and stew. There is a very old tradition that the herder should slash a cross on top of the loaf, and serve the first piece to his friend and helper, the sheep dog. Even today many Basque herders bake their bread in a pit under their cooking fire. They use a 5 qt. or 10" Dutch oven to bake in. Any lettering or numerals appear on the bread.

TO BAKE THE SHEEPHERDER BREAD

3 c. very hot water
1 c. sour dough starter, or 2 pkgs.
  dry yeast
1/2 c. butter or bacon drippings
9-9 1/2 c. all purpose flour,
  unsifted
1/3 c. sugar
salad oil
2 1/2 tsp. salt

Grease inside of Dutch oven and lid. In a large pan make a batter of hot water, sugar, butter and salt. Stir until butter melts, let cool and stir in yeast, 5 c. flour. Now use enough remaining flour to make a stiff dough. Turn dough out on floured surface and knead until smooth and satiny, about 15-20 mins. Add flour as needed to prevent sticking. Let rise until double in size. Place in Dutch oven and let rise until it lifts lid 1/2". Place in heated pit with lid on, cover with wet burlap and dirt. Build a fire with some good hot coals, now go about your business. When you return you have your bread. In home oven, use Dutch oven, but only bake 10-15 mins. with lid on and finish 35 mins. with lid off in a 375 deg. oven. Turn loaf out and allow to cool.

SOFT GINGER BREAD (19TH CENTURY)

6 c. flour, 3 c. molasses, 1 tsp. cream of tartar, 1 c. lard or butter, 2 eggs, 1 tsp. of (Your guess is as good as ours! We simply could not decipher the ingredient Jim Dempsey specified. Sorry about that.),and 2 tsp. ginger. Mix well, bake in oven. Excellent eating.

INDIAN FRY BREAD

4 c. flour
2 T. powdered milk
1 T. baking powder
1 1/2 c. warm water
1 tsp. salt

Put flour in pan or bowl, add baking powder, salt, and powdered milk. Mix all together. Pour warm water into mixture, hand mix until soft. Take a ball of soft dough, pat back and forth and pull until flat and round. Melt 1 c. of lard in deep skillet or Dutch oven, cut a short slash in the center of round or run finger through. Put dough into hot fat. Turn until brown on both sides. Roll in powdered sugar, cinnamon sugar, or with honey.

SKILLET BREAD

4 c. flour
2 T. sugar
2 T. baking powder
3/4 c. powdered milk
1 1/2 tsp. salt
1 c. drippings and margarine
1 tsp. cream of tartar

Cut drippings into flour until the consistency of fine meal, add water to make a thick dough. Lightly grease a fry pan, put out dough to a 1" thickness. Fry 8-10 mins. each side over low heat. This mix can be stored in a cool place for several weeks

SHAPE BLUE CORN BREAD

1 c. juniper ash
3 1/2 c. water
1 c. boiling water
6 c. blue cornmeal

Mix juniper ash and boiling water. Put 3 1/2 c. water in pot, bring to boil. Strain ashes into water. Stir, add cornmeal. Knead into soft dough, firm, shape into small round patties. Place on hot skillet or griddle. Brown both sides.

NOGALES SPOON BREAD

1 303 can cream style corn
1 tsp. salt
1 corn meal
1/2 tsp. baking soda
1/3 c. shortening or drippings, melted
1 4-oz. can green chilies, drained, chopped
2 eggs, beaten
1 1/2 c. grated longhorn cheese

Combine and mix first 6 ingredients. Using a 9"x9"x2" pan, pour half the batter into the greased pan, sprinkle with chilies and cheese. Pour in remaining batter. Sprinkle with remaining cheese. Bake at 400 degs. 45 mins. Cool 10 mins. before cutting. Accompany with salsa.

PITA BREAD OR TRENCHER FILLING

1 lb. hot venison sausage
2 tsp. oregano
1/2 c. chopped onion
1 c. shredded cheddar cheese
1 15-oz. can pizza sauce
1 c. shredded mozzarella cheese
3 Pita bread or 1 loaf French bread
green chilies for garnish

Fry meat and onions until meat is crumbly. Drain. Combine sausage mixture, pizza sauce, and oregano. Open Pita bread, place half the cheeses on one side, replace cover. Pour on cheese, then pizza sauce, garnish with chilies and or pimento strips, or cut French bread in half, lengthwise. Place cheese on halves, pour on sauce, garnish with chilies and/or pimento strips, olives. Bake at 375 degs. 10-12 mins. or until cheese is bubbly hot.

APACHE BEAN BREAD

2 c. corn meal
2 eggs
1 tsp. salt
1 1/2 c. milk
1 tsp. baking powder
2 c. pinto beans, cooked, drained

Mix together dry ingredients, add milk and beaten eggs. Stir in beans, and pour into greased pan. Bake at 450 degs. for 20 mins. or until brown.

BLUE CORNMEAL BREAD

Use same procedure as corn bread except shape into 2-3 loaves. Bake in hot coals 1 hr. Brush off ashes, wash off with wet cloth. Serve warm.

HOPI PIKI BREAD

1 c. juniper ash
1 c. boiling water
3 c. water
1 c. blue cornmeal

Mix juniper ash in boiling water. Put 3 c. water in a pot. Boil, strain juniper ash water into pot. Stir, add cornmeal. Stir, let cool. Spread on hot griddle or stone with palm of hand. Be sure the layer is very, very thin.

SKILLET CORN BREAD

2 pkgs. corn bread mix
2 T. butter

In heavy metal handled 10" cast-iron skillet, melt butter. Prepare corn bread mix according to package directions. Spoon butter into skillet. Cover loosely with foil, place over hot coals. Cook corn bread about 50 mins. or until golden brown. Serve with real butter and honey.

PORK AND PEA PUDDING

Soak the pork, which should not be a fat piece, overnight in cold water. In another pan put 1 qt. of dried pears. In the morning put on the pears to boil slowly until tender. Drain and rub through a colander, season with pepper and salt. Mix with them 2 T. butter and 2 beaten eggs. Heat all well together. Have ready a floured pudding cloth, and put the pudding into it. Tie it up, leaving room to swell. Put in warm not boiling water. With the pork, boil together 1 hr. Lay the pork in the center of the dish, turn out the pudding, slice and arrange about the meat. Serve with hot applesauce. (From an old roundup cook, Moses Dodran.)

CHUCK WAGON SUET PUDDING

1 c. chopped suet, pea-size
1 c. firm packed brown sugar
1 c. raisins
1 c. chopped mixed fruit, anything
   left over
1 c. chopped walnuts

Mix separately:

2 c. flour
1 tsp. cinnamon
1 tsp. allspice or ginger
1 tsp. nutmeg
1 tsp. salt
2 tsp. baking powder

Mix this batch with the fruit, gradually beat in 1 1/2 c. canned milk. Wet a flour sack in hot water, wring out, sprinkle well with flour, tie pudding in the sack, and lower into pot of boiling water. Let boil for 3 hrs. Keep water level above sack. Let drain for at least 1/2 hr. before untying sack. Turn pudding out on a dish. Chill and slice, serve with flavored hard sauce. This was called "Bastard In A Sack."

CARROT PUDDING

1 lb. grated carrots, 3/4 lb. chopped suet, 1/2 lb. each raisins and currents, 4 T. sugar, 8 T. flour, spices to suit your taste. Boil 4 hrs., place in oven 20 mins. Serve with wine sauce.

FRUIT VALISE PUDDING

1 qt. flour
1 salt spoonful salt
1 T. each lard and butter
2 c. milk or enough to make a soft
    dough
1 tsp. soda dissolved in boiling
    water
2 tsp. cream of tartar sifted
    through flour
1 qt. berries, fruit, apple, jam

Roll out crust 1/4" thick oblong shape. Cover thickly with fruit, sprinkle with sugar, begin at one end and roll it up closely with fruit inside. Putting this in leave a narrow margin, which should be folded down closely like the flap on a pocket book. Pinch the edges of the folded edge together to prevent escape of the fruit. Baste up in a bag the same size and shape as the valise. Dip bag in hot water, wring out. Flour inside before putting in the pudding. Boil 1 hr. 30 mins. Serve hot with sauce, cut in 1/2" slices.

HUCKLEBERRY PUDDING
(CHUCK WAGON STYLE)

1 pt. milk
1 salt spoonful salt
2 eggs
1 tsp. soda dissolved in boiling
    water
1 qt. flour or enough for a batter
1 qt. berries, well dredged in flour
1 gill bakers yeast

Make a batter of eggs, milk, flour, yeast, salt, soda, and set it to rise in a warm place, about 4 hrs. When you are ready to boil it, stir in the dredged fruit quickly and lightly. Boil in floured cloth for 2 hrs. Eat hot with white sauce.

YORKSHIRE PUDDING

1 pt. milk
2 c. flour
4 eggs, yolks and whites beaten
   separately
1 tsp. salt

Be careful when mixing not to have the batter too stiff. This is also called Auction Pudding. It is very palatable and popular, and not so rich as might be thought from the manner of baking. Should be yellow brown when done. Originally the pudding pan was set under the drip of a spitted venison or beef roast. Today, except during hunting season, we use beef dripping right enough but we boil the pudding or bake it in the oven, with frequent basting. Either way it's delicious.

INDIAN PUDDING

2 c. milk
1/8 tsp. baking soda
1/4 c. cornmeal
1 c. milk
1/4 c. sugar
1/4 c. molasses
1/2 tsp. salt
whipped cream
1/2 tsp. ginger
nutmeg
1/2 tsp. cinnamon

Preheat oven to 275 degs. In saucepan or double boiler, cook milk over low heat until hot. Add cornmeal a little at a time stirring constantly. Cook 15 mins. or until mixture thickens. Remove from heat. Mix together sugar, salt, ginger, cinnamon, and baking soda in small bowl. Stir into cornmeal. Add milk and molasses, blend thoroughly. Pour into 1 qt. casserole. Bake 2 hrs. Serve warm with whipped cream and nutmeg.

BASIC BANNOCK MIX

1 c. all purpose flour
1/4 tsp. salt
1 heaping tsp. baking powder
2 T. powdered milk

To use, simply add water to ingredients to make a soft dough. Mold into cake 1" thick with very little handling. Lay in skillet over coals until crust forms on bottom. Turn over, prop skillet at an angle to the fire exposing top to the fire to become a golden brown. Use twig to test. If dough clings, it needs more heat. After more cooking, you can thump the loaf; should sound hollow. 15 mins., more or less. This recipe is in 1-man proportions. May be prepared in advance and will keep over 6 weeks when sealed in plastic bags.

RAISIN NUT BANNOCK

1 c. Bisquick
1/2 handful broken nut meats
2 T. butter
1/2 handful raisins
salt, as desired
1 tsp. baking powder
water

Use enough water to make combined ingredients into a light dough. Pat out to a good-sized cake. Melt 1 T. butter in iron skillet. Place cake in center and cook until brown. Turn and brown the other side. Lean skillet at an angle to the fire after sprinkling cake with cinnamon sugar. When using a Dutch oven, heat the lid with the bottom. To bake your biscuits or bread it will take 6 good gray briquets or a shovelful of live coals underneath, and 12 briquets on the lid, or a good shovelful of coals on the lid. Add or detract as needed.

BANNOCK FOR ONE HUNTER

1 c. flour
1/4 tsp. salt
1 tsp. baking powder
enough water to form dough

Have a heavy skillet hot and greased, make a 1" thick cake. Leave a hole in the center, fry until crust forms on the bottom, flip and do that side the same. Roll in granulated sugar and cinnamon or as regular bread.

ACORN BANNOCK

3/4 c. flour
1 tsp. baking powder
1/2 c. ground acorn meal
1/4 tsp. salt

Add enough liquid to make a firm dough. Have fry pan hot and greased. Firm a cake about 1" thick. Cut hole in center, fry until bottom crust forms. Turn, serve hot (roll in sugar).

CHRISTMAS BANNOCK

Mix 1/2 c. ground nut meats, 1/2 c. raisins with 1 pkg. Bisquick Mix. Bake as trail bannock or wrap biscuits or loaf loosely in foil. Bake in coals 6 mins. Serve hot with jam or marmalade.

LEMON SAUCE

1 large c. sugar
1 lemon, all the juice, 1/2 grated
  peel
1/2 c. butter
1 tsp. nutmeg
1 egg
3 T. boiling water

Cream the butter and sugar, beat in the egg whipped light, the lemon and nutmeg. Beat hard 10 mins. and add a spoonful at the time of the boiling water, put in a tin pail, and set within the uncovered top of the tea kettle, which you must keep boiling until the steam heats the sauce very hot, but not boiling, stir constantly. Use the same for orange or lime.

HARD SAUCE
(CHUCK WAGON FARE)

Stir to a cream 1 c. butter
juice 1 lemon
3 c. powdered sugar
2 tsp. nutmeg

When light, beat in 3/4 teacup wine. Beat long and hard until several shades lighter in color than at first and creamy in consistency. Smooth into shape with a broad knife dipped in cold water; stamp with a wooden mold, first scaled then dipped in cold water. Set upon ice until pudding is served.

WHITE WINE SAUCE

1/2 c. butter
1/2 c. boiling water
2 1/2 c. powdered sugar
1 tsp. nutmeg
2 wine glasses pale sherry or white
  wine

Work the butter into the sugar, mixing as you go with boiling water. Beat long and hard until your bowl is nearly full of a creamy mixture. Then add gradually the wine and nutmeg, still beating hard. Turn into a tin pail set within a saucepan of boiling water and stir frequently until sauce is hot but not until it boils. Take the saucepan from the fire, leave the pail standing in the water, stir the contents now and then until you're ready to sauce the pudding. If made right, sauce will be milk white.

HARD SAUCE

Beat to a cream 1/4 lb. butter, add gradually 1/4 lb. sugar, beat it until very white, add a little lemon juice, or grate nutmeg on top.

BRANDY SAUCE

1/2 c. butter
1 wine glass brandy
3 c. powdered sugar
1 tsp. mixed cinnamon and mace

Warm butter slightly, work in sugar, and when this is light, the brandy and spice. Beat hard, shape into mold, keep in cold place until needed.

CREAM SAUCE

1 c. milk, 1 tsp. of flour and 1 T. of butter, salt and pepper. Put the butter in a small fry pan, and when hot, but not brown, add the flour, stir until smooth, then gradually add the milk, let it boil up once. Season to taste with salt and pepper and serve. Used for creamed potatoes, peas and onions, and other vegetables, omelets, fish, sweet breads, anything requiring a white sauce. If you have plenty of cream use it, and omit the butter.

PORT WINE SAUCE FOR GAME

Half a tumbler of currant jelly, half a tumbler of port wine. Half a tumbler of game stock, half a tsp. of salt, 2 T. lemon juice, 4 cloves, a speck of cayenne pepper. Simmer cloves and stock together for 1/2 hr., strain in other ingredients and let all melt together. Part of the gravy from the game roast may be used.

HORSE-RADISH SOUR CREAM SAUCE

    1 c. sour cream
    2 tsp. sugar
    3 T. prepared white horse-radish
    1 T. chives, fresh or dried

Combine all ingredients, blend well, chill until serving time. Serve with corned beef or venison, other canned meats, also ham and smoked loin.

IRON SKILLET BISCUITS

1 c. biscuit mix
1/2 c. powdered milk
2 tsp. baking powder
1 tsp. sugar
1 tsp. salt

With fork, cut in 2 T. bacon grease. Slowly add water until dough is soft enough to work with. Drop by tablespoon into hot greased skillet. Cover, turn when brown·

CORN MEAL FLAPJACKS (INDIAN MEAL)

1 qt. sour or buttermilk
2 tsp. molasses
2 eggs, beaten light
1 T. drippings or broth
1 tsp. salt
1/2 c. flour
1 tsp. soda dissolved in hot water meal to make a batter a trifle thicker than the usual pancake batter

Fry on hot greased griddle or in spider.

BLUEBERRY BUCKLE

Sift together 1/2 c. sugar, 2 c. flour, 3 T. baking powder, 1/4 tsp. salt. Separately beat 1 egg, 12 c. milk, 1/4 c. melted butter. Pour liquid into dry ingredients, stir just to mix. Spread in shallow baking dish 9"x9"x2", well greased. Cover with 1 pt. berries and 1 T. lemon juice. Top with a mixture 1/2 c. sugar, 1/3 c. flour, 1/2 tsp. cinnamon, 1/4 c. melted butter. Bake at 350 degs. 55-60 mins.

KIVA CORN DUMPLINGS

1 c. biscuit mix
1 can cream style corn
4 T. cornmeal

Drop batter by tablespoons on top of any stew, Mulligan, etc. Cook as any other dumplings. 10 mins. covered, 10 mins. uncovered.

HASTY DUMPLINGS

Mix pancake mix the usual way with minimum of water. Drop gobs of it into hot broth as soup and you will have gourmet dumplings. Very good in duck soup.

GINGERBREAD PANCAKES

1 1/2 c. biscuit mix
1 c. milk
1/4 tsp. ground ginger
1/4 c. light molasses
1/8 tsp. each ground nutmeg,
   cinnamon
1 T. melted margarine
1 egg, slightly beaten

Stir together biscuit mix, ginger, cinnamon, nutmeg. Combine the egg, milk, molasses and butter; add to dry ingredients, beat until smooth. Preheat your griddle or fry pan over med. heat, grease lightly as needed. For each pancake about 1/3 c. butter on the griddle, cook until brown and bubbles break on top. Turn and brown. About 14 4" cakes.

146

BEER SIGN (DOUGHNUTS)

Flour for sponge, 1 c. sugar, 2 eggs, 1/2 c. of shortening, 1 tsp. of soda, 1 c. sour milk, mix a soft dough, cut in rings, have your lard very hot, in which place a peeled potato to keep the lard from burning, drop in your rings, they will come to the top of your lard when light, fry to a nice brown. When taken out sprinkle cinnamon sugar on them.

CRUST FOR MEAT PIES

- 1 qt. flour
- 2 tsp. cream of tartar sifted into dry flour
- 3 T. lard
- 2 1/2 c. milk
- 1 tsp. salt
- 1 tsp. soda wet with hot water and stirred into milk

Work up very lightly and quickly. Do not get too stiff. Roll out and cut, or sheet as needed.

SKILLET CORN PONE

- 4 c. corn meal
- 1 1/2 tsp. salt
- 3 c. hot water

Mix together and stir vigorously. The harder you stir, the lighter your pone. Press into cakes about 1/2" thick, fry in a little hot bacon grease, about 12 mins.

JOHNNY CAKE

2/3 tsp. of soda, 3 T. sugar, 1 tsp. cream of tartar, 1 egg, 1 c. sweet milk, 6 T. Indian meal, 3 T. flour, a little salt. This makes a thin batter. Fry as you would hot cakes.

SMOKI CORN CAKES

2 1/2 c. cornmeal
2 eggs
6 tsp. baking powder
3 T. drippings or shortening
1/4 c. flour
2 1/2 c. milk
1 tsp. salt

Mix all ingredients until thoroughly blended.
Fry on greased griddle. Use bacon drippings.
Serve with powdered sugar, syrup, or honey.
Makes 36 cakes.

DOWN EAST GREEN CORN GRIDDLE CAKES

2 17-oz. cans cream style corn
2 egg whites, stiffly beaten
2 c. milk
1 tsp. salt
2 egg yolks
2 c. all purpose flour, unsifted
2 tsp. sugar
4 tsp. baking powder

In a bowl mix corn, milk, egg yolks, sugar,
salt. Stir in baking powder, fold in egg
whites; spoon batter, 1/4 c. at a time onto
lightly greased, preheated griddle; brown one
side, turn and brown the other side. Serve with
butter, honey, maple syrup, sausage. Serves 6.

ASH CAKES

1/2 c. chopped nut meats
1 c. biscuit mix
1/2 c. cornmeal
enough water to make firm dough

Form into biscuit size, place directly in
ashes. Turn once, serve hot. Try mixing crushed
walnuts and acorn meal. Real good!

DRAWN BUTTER

2 tsp. flour
1 teacup water or milk
1 1/2 ozs. butter
a little bit of salt

Put the flour and salt in a bowl and add a little at a time of the water or milk, working it very smooth as you go. Put into a tin cup and set in a vessel of boiling water. As it warms stir, and when it has boiled 1 min. or more, add the butter by degrees, stirring all the time until it is entirely melted and incorporated with the flour and water. Boil 1 min. Mix with milk when you use in puddings. Mix with water for meat or fish.

TO MAKE DRAWN BUTTER

Put 1/2 pt. milk in a perfectly clean stewpan, set it on a moderate fire. Put into a pt. bowl a heaping T. of wheat flour, 1/4 lb. butter, and a salt spoonful of salt, work these well together with the back of a spoon, then pour into it, stirring all the time in 1/2 pt. boiling water. When it is smooth stir it into the boiling milk. Let it simmer for 5 mins. or more and it is done. This recipe makes excellent drawn butter. To make less rich use less butter.

CRANBERRY-PINEAPPLE BUTTER

3 c. cranberries, 1 c. crushed pineapple, 3 1/2 c. sugar. Mix thoroughly, boil until thick, pour into sterilized jars, seal.

Notes

X

HodgePodge

RED
FLANNEL
STEW

RED FLANNEL STEW

2 tsp. bacon drippings
1/2 lb. cubed cheddar cheese
1 large onion, chopped
chili powder
2 c. cooked pinto beans
corn tortilla
1 c. corned beef
season to taste with salt, pepper
1 c. stewed tomatoes

Fry onions in bacon drippings. Add cooked beans. Mash into paste. Add remaining beans, meat, chili powder, seasoning and tomatoes. Heat, add cheese.

TERIYAKI MARINADE

1/2 c. soy sauce
2 cloves garlic, crushed
1/4 c. packed brown sugar
1/4 tsp. pepper
1 tsp. ground ginger
1/2 c. teriyaki sauce

Combine, mix well.

SWEET AND SOUR MARINADE

1 tsp. soy sauce
3/4 tsp. salt
1/2 c. vinegar
1/4 tsp. pepper
1/3 c. brown sugar
1 tsp. onion salt
1/2 c. pineapple juice
1 clove garlic, crushed

Combine and heat. Stir, cool, pour over meat or fish. Add fruit cocktail and thicken for sauce.

SHEEP'S HEAD BROTH

When the sheep is butchered, take the head to the blacksmith. There have it well seared, then have the butcher cut the head in half.

    1 sheep's head, cleaned
    3 ozs. barley
    1 pt. each diced carrots, turnips,
      leeks
    3 qts. water
    1 grated carrot

Remove the brain from the split skull, soak it in cold water and vinegar to blanch it. Soak the head in warm water and salt for 1/2 hr. Scrape the nostril bones, cleanse the head thoroughly. Blanch the head by placing in enough cold water to cover, then bring to boiling point. Then skimming it well, pour off the water. Put prepared head into a large soup pot. Cover with 3 qts. water, add the washed barley, bring to a boil, skim, add diced vegetables, season thoroughly and put to simmer gently 3-4 hrs., skimming if necessary. Add grated carrot 1/2 hr. before serving. When head is tender, lift out, add chopped parsley at the last, boil a few mins. Serve in hot tureen.

BRINE FOR CORNING

Mix 1 1/2 lbs. pickling salt (unoxidized), 1/2 lb. brown sugar, 1 oz. each cream of tartar, baking soda, and pickling spice in 1 gal. water, boiling hot. Allow to cool. Place meat in crock or tub, or granite ware. Pour brine over pieces of 1/2 to 1 lb.; take a week. Place these on top of your crock. Larger pieces require 10-14 days. Keep in temperature of 35-38 degs. In case scum or mold appears, remove meat, wash and replace with new brine.

CHUCK WAGON BEER CHILI

1 T. butter
1 1/2 tsp. chili powder
1 lb. ground venison
1/2 tsp. paprika
1 large onion, chopped
1 12-oz. can beer
1 303 can tomatoes
1 303 can kidney beans
1 6-oz. can tomato paste
1 tsp. salt
1/4 tsp. pepper

Melt butter in Dutch oven, add meat and onion. Cook until meat is lightly browned, stir frequently, add all other ingredients except beans; stir, cover. Simmer about 1 hr., stirring occasionally. Add beans, simmer 20 mins. longer. Stir frequently to keep from sticking. Serves 6.

JIM'S CHILI

3 lbs. ground venison
1 c. chopped parsley
1 mashed toe garlic
1 c. stuffed olives, quartered
1 c. celery, chopped, some leaves
1 tsp. each, chili powder, cayenne
   pepper
3 303 cans tomatoes
several dashes tabasco sauce
dash oregano
2 6-oz. cans tomato paste
1 large bay leaf

2 T. sugar
3/4 c. chopped onion
1 T. Worcestershire sauce

Coat meat with salt and pepper. Sauté meat with celery and garlic in bacon drippings or margarine; cover, simmer 10 mins. Stir occasionally, add tomatoes and paste, sugar, beans, salt and pepper, oregano, olives and Worcestershire sauce. Simmer about 10 mins. Taste, improve seasoning, cool, refrigerate over night, reheat and serve. Now you may add cooked red beans if desired.

SPICY MARINADE

2 T. water
1/4 tsp. pepper
1 T. steak sauce
1 tsp. salt
1 T. Worcestershire sauce
1/2 tsp. onion powder
2 T. soy sauce
1 clove garlic, crushed
1/2 tsp. liquid hickory smoke

Combine all ingredients. Pour over meat.

PEMMICAN

1 lb. jerky, pounded to meal
2 T. brown sugar
2 ozs. raisins
5 ozs. suet

Grind dry jerky several times until fine. For each lb. of jerky meat, add raisins and brown sugar. Blend well. Melt suet and stir in. The result when the suet hardens and cools is pemmican. There are many variations of this food. You may also use dried apples, ground nuts, prunes, dates, or dried mix. Whatever you use, it's a hunter's friend.

BOILED CALF'S HEAD

Calf's head, a little salt, water, 4 T. of melted butter, 1 T. minced parsley, pepper and salt to taste, 1 T. lemon juice. After the head has been skinned out and thoroughly cleaned, and the brain removed, soak it in warm water to blanch it. Lay the brain also in warm water to soak; let it remain about 1 hr. Put the head into a suitable size stew pot with sufficient water to cover it. When it boils, add a little salt, take off every particle of scum as it rises, and boil the head until perfectly tender. Boil the brain, chop it, mix with butter melted, minced parsley, pepper, salt and lemon juice in above proportions. Take up the head, skin the tongue, put it on a small dish, with the brain pieces around it. Have ready some butter and parsley. Smother the head with it; the remainder send to the table in a tureen. Bacon, ham, pickled pork, or a pig's cheek are indispensable with calf's head. The brain is sometimes chopped with hard boiled eggs.

MASHED POTATO DUMPLINGS

2 c. water
3 c. potato flakes
1 tsp. salt
2 T. margarine
1/2 c. hominy grits
3 eggs

In saucepan mix water, salt and grits; stir over low heat until the mixture boils and thickens. Remove from heat and stir in potato flakes. Mixture will be crumbly. Stir in butter, beat in eggs 1 at a time, shape mixture into 14 balls about the size of a large plum. Drop into boiling salt water or broth; simmer 15-20 mins. Drain. Serve with stews. Toasted buttered crumbs may be sprinkled over the dumplings at serving time.

VINEGAR PIE

In a dutch oven combine 4 c. white sugar, 2 1/2 c. water, 3/4 c. cider vinegar, 1/2 lb. real butter, nutmeg to taste, pinch of salt. Boil mixture. Make pie dough for a double crust, cut into strips, recross on top of solution. Let cool. Set up when cool.

IRISH WHISKEY PIE

3 egg yolks
3 egg whites
5 T. super fine sugar
1 c. heavy cream, whipped
1 pkg. unflavored gelatin
3 T. Irish whisky
1 tsp. instant coffee
1 tsp. vanilla extract
1 T. boiling water
8" chocolate cookie crumb crust pie
    shell
1 c. light cream

Combine egg yolks and sugar in mixing bowl until light and in saucepan dissolve gelatin and coffee in 1 T. boiling water; stir in light cream, bring to a boil over low heat, lower temperature, pour in egg yolks and sugar mixture, stirring constantly until thick. Remove from heat and allow to cool. In a large bowl beat egg whites to soft peaks, fold in 1/2 c. whipped heavy cream (save rest for garnish), whiskey and vanilla. Fold in cooled egg yolk mixture and pour into baked 8" pie shell. Makes 8 portions.

TO MAKE COFFEE

1/2 pt. fresh ground coffee
white of an egg, crushed shell of
   same
1 qt. boiling water
1/2 c. cold water to settle same

Stir up the egg shell and beaten egg white with the coffee and a very little cold water, mix gradually with boiling water in pot. Stir from sides and top as it boils up. Boil pretty fast for 12 mins., pour in cold water and take from the fire. Set gently on the hearth to settle. In 5 mins. pour it carefully into your cups.

PIONEER COUGH SYRUP

Add 3/8 oz. each of aniseed, stick or root licorice and senna leaf to 1/2 pt. boiling water. Simmer, reduce to 1/2 pt. and strain. When cool add 1/2 pt. simple syrup and 1/2 pt. rum or good whiskey. Take often.

POSSE STEW

2 cans whole corn
1 large can hominy
1 large can tomatoes
2 large cans ranch style beans
1 green chili
1 lb. hamburger (or choice of game
   meat)
1 large onion

Cook hamburger with onion; drain off fat; then mix all ingredients together in large stew pot. Serve hot with corn bread. Many folks claim this is the best stew around.

SON-OF-A-BITCH STEW

It is said there are as many recipes for this dish as there are cooks to make it. In the days of the big round-up it was a chuck wagon delicacy. No two batches were ever alike. You don't really make it. You just use whatever is at hand and it grows. Usually a pot is started when a calf is killed and butchered. The first thing you do is take the steaks and roast and other choice cuts and throw all the rest except the hide, horns and belly into the pot, along with tongue, heart, liver, sweetbreads and anything else you want. Add some potatoes, carrots, tomatoes, canned corn, onions. Now add some water and simmer slowly for a good long time, the longer the better. Just before serving pour in a bottle of cooking sherry.

NAVAJO BACKBONE STEW

4 c. fresh corn
2 tsp. salt
4 c. water
10 pieces backbone, big horn, lamb,
    or mutton

Put corn and water in pot, stir. Add backbone pieces, salt. Cook 1 hr.

ROSE PETAL JELLY

Pick red roses early in the day, wash thoroughly, pick off petals and cut off rose base. Drain on a towel, pack lightly 1 c. petals, add 1 c. water, 2 tsp. lemon juice. Boil until petals are a washed-out pink. Drain petals, reserving liquid, 3/4 T. for each T. liquid. Boil until scum rises to the top. Skim off scum, pour jelly into hot sterilized glasses, seal, store.

COURT BOUILLON

1/4 c. vinegar or lemon juice
2 large green peppers
6 c. water
1 large onion, sliced
1 large carrot, sliced
1 T. pickling spice in cheesecloth
2 celery stalks with leaves
1/2 tsp. salt

Combine all ingredients in deep saucepan, bring to boil, reduce heat. Cook gently 15 mins. Remove spice at your discretion, cool. Makes 1 1/2 qts.; for robust flavored fish.

SEAL LIVER LOAF

1/4 lb. salt pork
2 eggs, slightly beaten
1 lb. seal liver, soaked overnight
1 T. minced onion
1 1/2 c. hot water
1 tsp. poultry seasoning
1 c. cracker crumbs
salt and pepper

Fry pork, remove, add liver and brown both sides. Grind pork and liver coarse. Pour water over cracker crumbs. Combine meat, crumbs, eggs, onion, seasoning. Place in greased casserole, bake at 375 degs. 40 mins. Serves 6.

WATER CRESS SALAD

Gather enough water cress for 4 portions. Tear in pieces 1/2 small head lettuce, wedge 2 fresh tomatoes, 2 shallots sliced, season with salt, pepper, 1/8 tsp. paprika (Emerald Green dressing) or 3 T. salad oil, 2 T. vinegar and water, 1/2 tsp. sugar. Serve cold and crisp. Lemon juice may be used in place of vinegar.

EMERALD GREEN SALAD

    1 c. salad dressing
    2 drops liquid hot sauce
    1/4 c. sour cream
    2 tsp. water
    1 hard boiled egg, peeled, chunked

Combine all ingredients in blender, mix until thoroughly blended. Makes 1 1/2 c., 2 tsp. per serving.

Notes

Secrets of Hunters and Trappers

SECRETS OF HUNTERS AND TRAPPERS

A good lure for foxes, mink, sable, martin, wolves, bears, wildcats is to take one-half pound strained honey, one-quarter dram of musk, three drams of lavender, and four pounds of tallow. Mix the whole thoroughly together and make it into forty pills or balls. Place one of these pills under the pan of each trap when setting it.

To catch foxes:

Take equal amounts oil of amber and beaver oil. Rub over the trap. Bait with fish or bird. Set in the usual way.

To catch mink:

Follow same procedure for catching foxes.

To catch muskrats:

In the female muskrat near the vagina is a small bag that holds about thirty to forty drops of liquid. Now, all the trapper has to do is catch a few female muskrats and squeeze the contents of the bags into a vial. When in quest of muskrats, sprinkle a few drops of liquid on the bushes over and around the trap. This will attract the male muskrats in large numbers, and if the traps are properly arranged, large numbers of muskrats can be taken.

In trapping muskrats, steel traps should be used and they should be set in the paths and runs of the animals where they come up on the banks, and in every case the traps should be set under water and carefully concealed. Care should be taken that there is sufficient chain to enable the animals to reach water after being caught; otherwise they are liable to escape by tearing or gnawing off their legs.

To catch beaver:

In trapping for beavers, set the trap at the edge of the water or dam at the point where the animals pass from deep to shoal water, and always beneath the surface, and fasten it by means of a stout chain to a picket driven into the bank or to a bush or tree. A flat stick should be made fast to the trap by a cord a few feet long, which would, if the animal carried away the trap, float on the water and point out the positions. The trap should then be baited with a preparation called "Beaver Medicine."

"MADSTONES"

From early history madstones have been used and are used even today. At one time they were used on all poisonous bites, even those of mad dogs.

Madstones are very poisonous and seldom larger than a silver dollar. They look like any common stone, but that's where the similarity ends. They are certainly not common. They are found occasionally in the gut of certain animals: goats, porcupines in old Europe; monkeys in Africa; albino deer in North America.

The madstone was applied directly to the wound and stuck there. When saturated with blood and poison it was removed and cleaned in sweet milk. If the milk turned light green it indicated the presence of poison, and meant further treatment was needed — all day if necessary — until the milk remained white.

THE ROUND-UP COOK

A good round-up cook had to be versatile, an expert at improving, inventing and making do with what was at hand in the chuck wagon. Most of the fruit was dried; for seasoning he had cinnamon, a couple bottles of vanilla, cooking wine and whiskey, salt, pepper, dried chili peppers, molasses.

He built something from nothing and got away with it. Fresh berries were a godsend. Dough boiled in the berry juice was called berry pot pie. There were also dumplings cooked in the juice and then poured over the berries. If raspberries were used, for example, it was called "Raspberry Fool."

Dutch oven deep pie was another standby. Berries were cooked and a biscuit dough baked on them and served. Sour dough biscuits and bread were baked in Dutch ovens. Beans were baked in buried Dutch ovens and called "bean-hole beans."

He drew as much respect as the trail boss — the Round-Up Cook.

HOW THE OLD TIMERS MEASURED

I was once told how the old timers measured in comparison to the measurements we use today:

1 pinch = a darn little bit
1 teaspoon = a little bit
1 tablespoon = a good bit
1 cup = a heap
4 cups = a heap
1 quart = another heap
1 gallon = 4 heaps
1 peck = 8 heaps
1 bushel = too damn much
1 dash = 2-3 drops
3 teaspoons = 1 tablespoon
16 tablespoons = 1 cup
1 cup = 8 fluid ounces
2 cups = 1 pint
4 cups = a quart
4 quarts = 1 gallon
8 quarts = 1 peck
4 pecks = 1 bushel

Then there were the recipes that used the handful and a dusting of seasoning, a salt spoon-

166

ful, a squirt of something or other, a tea-cupful and a coffee cupful.

ASTHMA CURE

Get a tanned muskrat skin and wear it over the lungs with the fur side next to the body. It will bring certain relief.

HOMEMADE HARD SOAP

Pour 12 quarts soft boiling water on two-and-one-half pounds of unslaked lime. Dissolve five pounds of Sal Soda in 12 quarts soft hot water, then mix and leave everything alone for 12 to 24 hours. Pour off all the clear liquid, being careful not to allow any of the sediment to run off. Boil three-and-one-half pounds clean grease and three or four ounces of resin in the lye, until the grease disappears. Pour into a suitable container and let it stand a day to stiffen, then cut into the size soap bars you want.

It is well to put the lime in all the water and then add the soda. After pouring off the fluid, add two or three gallons of water. Let it stand with the lime and soda dredges a day or two. This makes an excellent washing fluid to boil or soak the clothes in. Use one pint in a boiler of water.

USE CARBIDE LAMP INSTEAD

A carbide lamp is recommended instead of a bulky lantern. The lamp and fuel are both compact and will last a long time.

BITES OF DOGS
Modern remedy: seek medical advice
The only safe remedy in case of a bite from a dog suspected of madness is to burn out the

wound thoroughly with a red hot iron or with lunar caustic for fully eight seconds so as to cauterize the entire surface of the wound. Do this as soon as possible. For no time is to be lost. It will be expected that the parts touched with the caustic will turn black.

WEATHERPROOFING LEATHER

Melt one cup tallow and one-fourth cup beeswax over a low flame, then blend one-half cup castor oil. After this is done add one-half ounce jet black; let cool and apply to leather.

To clean mildewed leather wipe with a solution of equal parts denatured alcohol and water; dry in open air. If leather still looks spotty, clean with saddle soap, and in the case of luggage and shoes, finish with a good wax polish.

MORE SOAP: THE PIONEER WAY

Pioneer Soap No. 1

Save your surplus grease and animal fat. To two pounds of such add one-half can lye, two quarts of water. Let soak three days in an old enamel pot. Then add two-and-one-half quarts water and cook about thirty minutes or until lumps dissolve. Stir with wooden paddle to help break up lumps. Allow to stand overnight; cut out congealed mixture in bar-sized chunks. Lay aside on a log or rock to dry.

Pioneer Soap No. 2

Dissolve one can lye in seven cups cold water; cook and while still hot add about four pounds clean deer, elk, etc., tallow, cut into small chunks. Add one-fourth box borax, one-half cup household ammonia, one cup Clorox. Let mixture stand two days or until it is granulated. Stir

once in awhile with a wooden paddle, break up
lumps. Resulting soap will resemble cottage
cheese curd. May be run through fine good
grinder to make fine granules.

Pioneer Soap No. 3

Save wood ashes using an old wooden cask or old
pot with holes in the bottom. Pour boiling
water over ashes, saving draining liquid. Mix
liquid with cooking grease or render out fats
and trimmings. The potash lye liquid is cooked
with about one-third less grease than liquid
until water evaporates; stir occasionally.
When done remove from fire. Allow to set overnight, skim off soft soap. Hardwood ashes make
the best lye.

BUCKSKIN TANNING

Carefully skin out the animal, flesh real good,
grain. To grain a skin you need a beam made
from a hardwood log eight feet long and eight
inches in diameter, and free of knots. At one
end bore two one-and-one-half inch holes for
legs. Smooth off the high end for about three
feet. To make a graining knife, use a flat bar
of steel with square edges or an old worn out
file will do. Skin must be thoroughly soaked
before graining.

To flesh, hang hide on large flat surface.
In graining, push knife away from you. Start
at the neck. Two hands full of slack lime and
enough warm water to cover will soak hair
loose; leave twenty-four hours.

After graining, wash in clear water and use
soap suds and work about a half-hour to remove
lime. Your tanning solution will be one tablespoon of white vitriol, alum and salt.
Dissolve in enough water to cover the hide.
Soak twenty-four hours, remove, wring as dry

as possible. Hang in the sun and apply a half pint of Curriers oil or butter. Let hang two days. Remove to a flat surface and scrub with soapsuds and brush and plenty of arm muscles.

To get the color, hang over a smudge fire of rotten hardwood for about one full day. Confine smoke, pull and work skin over beam to make it pliable.

MORE ON TANNING No. 1

Skin out cat-size animal, flesh hide real good, soak six to eighteen hours according to weight of skin; soak in four gallons of cold, soft water, one-half ounce borax, one-half pint salt, one ounce sulfuric acid. Then wring dry, put into a solution of two gallons water, one-fourth pound pulverized oxalic acid, one quart salt. Leave about two full days. Remove, wring dry, hang in cool, shady place. Pull all ways while skin is drying. To proof against moths, use a stiff brush, and brush paris-white through hair.

MORE ON TANNING No. 2

Skin and flesh real good. Soak skin four to six hours in solution of one-fourth ounce borax, one-fourth cup salt, two gallons cold water. Remove and wring dry. Do not twist too tight. Make a solution of one-fourth pound powdered alum, one-half ounce borax, dissolved in hot water. Add sufficient rye meal to make a thick paste, spread thickly on flesh side, hang in cool shady place for about two weeks. Then work over the beam to soften it up. Brush paris-white through hair with a stiff brush.

GAME MEAT COOKING TIME

Buffalo, Bear . . . 45 mins. for each 5 lbs.
Venison . . . 1 hr. for each 4 lbs.

Woodchuck, Wild Boar . . . 3/4 hr. per 5 lbs.
Old Tough Rabbit . . . 1-1/2 hrs.
Young Rabbit . . . 1 hr.
Guinea Hen . . . 1 hr.
Large Duck . . . 3/4 hr.
Small Duck, Pigeon . . . 1 hr.
Grouse, Snipe . . . 1/2 hr.
Small birds such as Dove, Quail, Blackbird,
Robin . . . 15-20 mins.
Partridge, Pheasant, Prairie Hen . . . 1/2 to
3/4 hr.

NEW KETTLES

The best way to prepare a new kettle for use
is to fill it with clean potato peelings, boil
them for an hour or more. Then wash the kettle
with hot water. Wipe it dry, and rub it with
a little lard, repeat rubbing half a dozen
times after using. In this way you will prevent
rust and all the little annoyances liable to
occur in the use of new kettles.

NEW SKILLETS OR SPIDERS

Wash utensil well in hot water. Dry inside and
out. Now rub lard on all parts of the utensil.
Have a hot, clear fire, place skillet or spider
on the coals, allow to get very hot, remove and
allow to cool. When just warm again, rub all
over with lard, set aside to get cold. It is
then ready for use. Keep clean and oiled and
you have a friend.

GOLD PAN OVEN

Using your tin plate or a pie plate, place your
roast on it well greased. Rake away coals,
place pan on hot ground. Put gold pan over
roast, bank hot coals around and over it. Cook
about twenty-five minutes per pound. Turn
roast once. Try a pie or biscuits this way.

TO ROAST GAME BIRDS OR WATER FOWL

Have a bright, clean and steady fire for roasting fowl. Prepare bird as directed. Spit it, put a pint of hot water in the drippings pan, add to it a small tablespoon of salt and a small teaspoon of pepper. Baste frequently. Let it roast quickly without scorching.

When nearly done, put a piece of butter the size of a large egg in the water in the pan; when it melts baste with it. Dredge a little flour over it, baste again. Now let it finish.

Half an hour will roast a full grown pheasant, if the fire is right. When done take it up. Let the giblets (heart, liver, gizzard) boil tender, then chop them very fine, then put them in the gravy. Add a tablespoon of browned flour, and a bit of butter. Stir it over the fire for a few minutes, then serve in a gravy tureen. Giblets may be left to roast if desired.

FIELD DRESSING BIG GAME

You have made a good shot. Make sure your animal is dead. Position animal to allow guts to roll down the hill and cut. Cut around anus and tie off. Get your animal open and cleaned without puncturing any organs.

Begin on lower belly for first cut. Carefully slice open up to sternum. Skin out genitals. Tie off tube and lay aside. Now the abdominal wall is exposed so carefully pierce. Insert two fingers and follow so as not to puncture organs.

Continue up to sternum. Carefully cut around anus from outside to prevent contamination then tie off. Pull through pelvis for removal.

With cavity open and anus freed, tilt carcass allowing innards to be pulled out then scoop out any contaminates quickly. Next split the pelvis carefully with a heavy knife or belt ax. Carefully remove the bladder which lies just beneath the arch. The urethra is already tied off. Now simply pinch off the other tube. Trim away attaching tissue and lift bladder clear of the carcass.

Finally open the sternum by cutting along a center line with heavy knife or ax. Deer can be opened with a knife. Larger game will require an ax or saw to do the job. Reach as far up as possible in the throat and pull in on the windpipe and esophagus and sever both as far up as possible. Now pull out lungs, etc. Save the liver, heart, kidneys and tongue. Wipe out cavity with grass or toweling. If water is used sparingly, dry very carefully.

HINTS FOR COOKING BIG GAME PARTS

The liver, heart, kidneys, tongue were considered a prize delicacy by our pioneer fathers. These four parts may be eaten right away. They need no aging.

Often the liver was cooked over the camp fire while the rest of the carcass was being dressed out. The deer liver should be cooked as soon as possible after the kill. Cook medium rare. Liver becomes tough and rubbery when fried too long. Slice thin and sear on both sides in very hot butter or bacon grease. Salt and pepper to taste and serve immediately.

OLD, TOUGH LIVER

If deer is old or tough, brown the liver (do not slice until cooked) on all sides in butter or bacon grease. Add onions, one-half cup red wine, one-fourth cup water, one teaspoon vinegar. Cover and simmer for one hour or until tender. Just before removing from heat, season with salt and pepper. Slice thinly and serve hot or cold.

COOKING SMALL GAME

Small game should be prepared using dry heat, as roasting, broiling, pan broiling and frying. Dry heat cooking develops and preserves the good game flavor almost always. Even the plumpest, youngest small game may be protected from drying out by larding during cooking.

Frequent basting should accompany dry heat cooking to assure tender and juicy meat. Older animals that are less tender and tougher are best cooked in moist heat. These methods include braising, stewing and simmering.

It is useless to try roasting a tough oldster. Most always it will turn out tough, dry and tasteless. Moist cooking tenderizes and breaks down the connecting tissues. Seasonings added during moist cooking cause strong flavors to decrease. Moist heat cooks the game in steam from its own juices with a little liquid added. It simmers the meat just below boiling in hot liquid that may or may not cover the meat.

PLUCKING

Game birds have a tendency to be dry because they are much leaner than the domestic fowl. A plucked skin helps keep the meat moist and tender during cooking. Plucking is easiest when the bird is still warm. It has been found that dry plucking preserves the skin and makes for better eating.

Skin the birds when they are old and tough. Skinning is also advised on fishy ducks, coots and mud hens. Always cook skinned birds with the moist method.

FIELD DRESSING GAME BIRDS

Most important to sweet meat is the removal of the intestines and craw. Cut from breast bone to vent. Cut around vent, insert two fingers and gently twist and pull. Save heart, gizzard, and liver, when not too badly shot up. Make another cut along the underside of the bird's neck. Take out the craw and windpipe, and remove oil sacs from base of tail. This takes less than five minutes. Hang bird from your belt. Don't cram it into a game pocket with others to sour and spoil.

FIGURING AGE OF UPLAND GAME BIRDS

Many are the indications of birds' ages. Young game birds in prime condition are heavy for their size with round, firm breasts and clear skin. The skin on a young bird's feet is lighter in color. Its claws are sharp and the beak is flexible. Old birds have hard skin on their feet along with dull, blunted claws and a hard, inflexible beak.

Young birds have a small pointed pin feather at each wing tip, which is lost at the end of the first year. Blood will show when feather is pulled.

Individual telltale signs are shown in each species. Water fowl with even one V notched feather in the tail is young. Older birds have rounded or pointed feather tips.

Young wild turkeys have tail feathers protruding beyond the others. A pheasant is young if its spurs are dull, stubby and light colored, or if its tail feathers are short or the breast bone is pliable. Older birds have long, sharp, glossy, dark spurs. The breast bone of a young partridge will break easily and the leg will be plump near the foot.

COOKING TIME FOR SMALL GAME

Cooking time influences the tenderness, juiciness and flavor of small game. Over-cooking makes game tough, dry and unpalatable. Prolonged cooking should be avoided. Cook until well done but not overdone.

Larding and basting with drippings or additional fat in roasting or broiling shortens the cooking period and increases the good flavor that is locked in fat.

SOAKING AND MARINATING

Soaking, marinating and parboiling will remove strong tastes and tenderize meat but should be avoided with small game when possible. Young, well conditioned small game should never be subjected to these methods since protein, minerals and vitamins are reduced as toughness and strong flavors are reduced. Rabbits and squirrels will almost never need special preparation, except where the carcass has been poorly bled.

SIX MOST POPULAR SMALL GAME ANIMALS

The six most popular small game animals are rabbit, squirrel, raccoon, opossum, beaver, and musquash (muskrat).

These are closely followed by the woodchuck, porcupine, lynx (bobcat) prairie wolf (coyote), skunk, and javelina.

A woodchuck (ground hog) can weigh twenty-five pounds, but the average is about ten pounds. The woodchuck is of the squirrel family. The meat is dark and tender and usually tasty because it feeds on vegetables and grasses.

Porcupine is usually considered an emergency survival food. It is a true vegetarian and can be eaten if all fat is removed.

Lynx (bobcat, cougar) are all said to be and are delicious eating. They are reputed to have been the favorite game meal of many Indian tribes and among the mountain men and early fur traders.

Prairie wolf (coyote) ranges from Costa Rica to Alaska and all of the United States. It is eaten in times of famine.

Skunk, after the infamous scent gland and all fat are removed, is delicious eating. The scent glands on either side of the rectum when removed leave the meat sweet and tender.

Javelina is a small forty to sixty-five pound relative of the wild boar and ranges in Texas, New Mexico and Arizona. Its meat is dry, porklike and light. The meat is barbecued or spit roasted with a good basting sauce.

The average dressed weight of a cottontail is one-and-one-half pounds. Its meat is white and tender, slightly gamy.

Squirrels range in weight (grays) from six to twelve ounces; foxes from eight ounces to one-and-one-half pounds. Meat is light red to pink; usually very tender and of good flavor. An older squirrel can be as tough as an old shoe sole. The meat becomes dark red as the animal ages. A squirrel that has been feeding on corn and hickory nuts has a flavor all its own and requires no seasoning. Fried like chicken at this stage is the usual cooking method. It goes well with gravy and biscuits.

The muskrat has several names. They are marsh hare, marsh rabbit, and musquash. This animal is clean, living mainly on rushes, cattail, and other water plants around water. It is widely distributed across the United States, living in stabilized bodies of water. Its meat is sweet and tender with dark red, soft, short fiber and has a pronounced wild taste. Bloody or strong carcasses should be soaked in vinegar brine overnight, changing solutions a couple of times. Remove all fat. Parboiling sometimes helps reduce the strong flavor in older animals. After this it may be broiled, fried, roasted or braised.

Sometimes raccoon is strong flavored. The coon is a very clean animal in habits and diet.

Its food consists mainly of crayfish, frogs, insects, berries and corn. There are a few that raid garbage cans but the ones that do are in the minority. The raccoon belongs to the bear family. It lays up during the day; roams and feeds at night; loves swamps and marshy land. At full maturity a raccoon can weigh twenty-five pounds. The best eating one weighs ten to twelve pounds. Old coons are strong in taste and are tough. The young coon is best to eat. The meat is dark red, coarse and long fibered. It is sweet and porklike in flavor, not as rich and not quite as fat. The strong flavor is in the fat. So remove the fat. Remove the scent kernels under the front legs and in the meaty parts of the hind legs. Lard and baste while cooking.

Index

Charles G. Irion is the author and founder of Irion Books (www.irionbooks.com) which includes *Remodeling Hell, Autograph Hell, Car Dealer Hell* and soon-to-be-released *Divorce Hell*. Charles has also authored the long-awaited Summit Murder series, which includes 3 novels: *Murder on Everest, Abandoned on Everest*, and *Murder on Elbrus*. As an explorer, Irion has visited more than 60 countries and is an accomplished SCUBA diver. He participated in a 1987 expedition to Mount Everest from the China side. Irion holds a Masters of Business Administration in International Marketing and Finance from The American Graduate School of International Management, and Bachelor of Arts degrees in both Biology and Economics from the University of California, Santa Barbara. A successful investor and businessman, Irion is founder of U.S. Park Investments, a company that owns and brokers manufactured home and RV communities. He is also the founder of a children's dictionary charity, a founding member of Phoenix Social Venture Partners and past president of a local Lions Club.

RV Resorts Recommended in Arizona:

www.meridianrvresort.com
www.ponderosarvresort.com
www.heberrvresort.com

Other Books by Charles G. Irion

The "Hell" Series

CAR DEALER HELL

The Truth
About Deception

www.cardealerhellthebook.com

AUTOGRAPH HELL

It Doesn't Have to
Be Real, It Just
Has to Be Authentic

www.autographhell.com

REMODELING HELL

How the Unpredictable Demons of Remodeling
and Construction Taught Expensive, Hellish
Lessons to a Trusting Guy

www.remodelinghellthebook.com

The Summit Murder Series

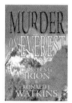

**MURDER ON
EVEREST**

by Charles G. Irion
& Ronald J. Watkins

www.murderoneverest.com

**ABANDONED ON
EVEREST**

True Story of Derek
Sodoc's Death!
by Quentin Stern

www.abandonedoneverest.com

"A New Kind of Murder Novel"
www.summitmurderseries.blogspot.com

www.irionbooks.com
www.twitter.com/CharlesIrion